Readers' Comments

 S0-AFG-658

Thanks so much for sharing your meditation book with me. I found myself falling into a deep blissful state after reading it!
Carol Susan Roth, *Literary agent. USA*

Dada has a rare quality of conveying some of the world's deepest truths in simple, clear language. He takes us into the depths of a rich world of deeper spiritual realities, but he always takes us by the hand so we never stray too far from its eloquently simple message; it is this balance that Dada strikes which makes this book a must-read for anyone even remotely interested in the practice of meditation.
New Renaissance Magazine. *UK*

Dada Nabhaniilananda's voice is that of a wise, courteous and truthful friend. He explains meditation without stripping away its mystery.
Sparrow, *Poet and author of Republican Like me; Yes, You ARE a Revolutionary; America: A Prophecy. USA*

Whether you are a complete beginner or an accomplished practitioner, this book is sure to make you want to just sit down and close your eyes.
Devashiish Donald Acosta, *Author of Devi, Anandmurti – The Jamalpur Years and When the Time Comes. Puerto Rico*

I congratulate Dada Nabhaniilananda for his enlightening and beautifully inspiring book on spiritual meditation as taught in his sacred tradition of Tantra – free of jargon and obscuring concepts, always direct, straight-talking and to the heart of the matter. Dada has in a masterful stroke answered many common questions on meditation, given useful tips and guidelines on how to practice interspersed with his subtly humorous stories, and clarified for the reader the essence of meditating with profundity and practicality. Not only does he share with us the fine nuances of mantra meditation, he goes further than many current authors on meditation by offering us a glimpse into the social dimensions of genuine spirituality. This is a personally and socially transformative book.
Chris Kang *PH.D. (Studies in Religion), Co-Author of The Meditative way: Readings in the Theory and Practice of Buddhist Meditation. Australia*

This is an easy to read, easy to understand illuminating book on meditation. I strongly recommend it for the new practitioner or the seasoned meditator. It is full of insights. Transformative.
Professor Sohail Inayatullah, *Tamkang University. Taiwan*

This is the very book which opened my eyes to spirituality and started my journey of self discovery. The devotional sentiment and the clean logic in the book evoked the yearning for spirituality inside me. Now I've been on the path for 7 years and each step takes me to a new scene. But I can never forget the book which leaded me (sic) to the first step. I am truly grateful to Dada, and his book.
I'm glad that the book is also in Chinese now.
Lina Wang, *USA*

Your book is a great little book. It gives a good introduction to meditation. Lively anecdotes from the author's own experience bring it alive and lead the readers to the feeling, "well, if he can do it, so can I"!
Malati, *India*

"This is a wonderfully comprehensive and accessible introduction to meditation and the way that Dada effortlessly leads the reader through what are pretty sophisticated concepts is impressive indeed. It has no doubt had a large part to play in my own personal progress of the last week or so."
John Hills, *UK*

We are so inspired by your book "Close your eyes & Open your mind." Now all the Chinese translation has been done. Thank you so much.
Sanjaya, *Taiwan*

What joy to read your book. It's clear and so well said. It brings to mind all kinds of memories. Words that are written in my universal mind so to speak. And with touches of delightful humour.
Sherill, *USA*

CLOSE YOUR EYES & OPEN YOUR MIND
A Practical Guide to Spiritual Meditation

DADA NABHANIILANANDA

CLOSE YOUR EYES & OPEN YOUR MIND

A Practical Guide to Spiritual Meditation

DADA NABHANIILANANDA

CLOSE YOUR EYES & OPEN YOUR MIND
A Practical Guide to Spiritual Meditation

DADA NABHANIILANANDA

Published by Innerworld Publications
San German, Puerto Rico
To contact publisher, to order or for copyright permissions
please go to www.innerworldpublications.com

Distributed by Eternalwave: www.eternalwave.com

©Dada Nabhaniilananda 2012
All Rights Reserved

Library of Congress Control Number: 2012934900
ISBN 978-1-881717-08-9

Cover design: **Shivaru**

Layout: **Jagadiish**

Back cover photo: **Anirvan**

Chakra illustration: **Jagadiish**

Dedication

To an old friend,
without whom this book would never have been written.

Acknowledgements

Firstly I would like to thank all my meditation students who, over the years, inspired me with their sincerity and insightful questions, and helped me to understand how to teach this subject more effectively.
Many others have helped with this book and I
cannot mention them all, but of particular note are:
Jayanta Kumar, Malati, Devashiish, Dada Jyotirupananda,
Geoff Hooper, Krsna Deva, Phanendra, Manorainjan,
Dada Giridevananda, Dada Maheshvarananda, Amal, Giridhara,
Mahadeva, Rajiva, Jyotirmaya, John Hills, Ac. Devanistha,
Dada Jagadiishananda, Jagadiish, Bhakti Devi,
Dada Gunamuktananda, Gretchen Vogel, Brian Knittel,
Maggie Finefrock, Viveka McEwen, Faye Bright, Vishvarupa,
Shiva Singh & Arati.
I'd also like to thank my Acarya who first taught me meditation, and
Dada Cidanandaji who taught me more.

And thanks, above anyone,
to my Guru Shrii Shrii Anandamurti
– there are some debts you can never repay.

Table of Contents

Introduction

"Your vision will become clear only when you look into your heart. Who looks outside, dreams. Who looks inside, awakens."
Carl Jung

New Zealand, 1975. I started practicing meditation and my friends concluded that I had finally lost my last marble. It seemed as though I was about the only person on planet Earth who was into this stuff. I felt like an alien.

Never one to shy away from being different I followed my heart and ended up going to India to train as a meditation teacher. In 1979, I was ordained as an Acharya (a yoga monk and spiritual teacher).

Times sure have changed. Nowadays everyone seems to think that meditation is wonderful. Expensive advertising campaigns featuring images of slender ladies meditating promote airlines, clothing, furniture, legal services—even meditation. After a 7000 year history of people meditating and feeling more serene and calm, doctors and scientists produce lengthy research papers 'proving' that meditation makes you feel serene and calm. Not only does meditation work in practice—it works in theory as well!

And for anyone who thinks meditation is a bit wimpy, did you know that Wolverine from the X-Men films meditates? At least Hugh Jackman, who plays him, does. As of course does Yoda, the Jedi Master.

> Finally, meditation is cool.

And let us not presume that all the Hollywood stars hanging out with the Dalai Lama are just forlorn planets hoping to catch a little reflected love. It turns out that many of them actually practice meditation themselves. What was an oddity back in 1975 when I was at the beginning of my journey is now more than just OK. Finally, meditation is cool.

So Why has Meditation become so Widely Accepted?

1. It reduces stress and promotes good health. Growing numbers of doctors and scientists recognize the beneficial physiological effects of meditation, especially in relation to stress relief and relaxation. Extensive mainstream research and documentation substantiates the significant health benefits of meditation. Even Kaiser Permanente health insurance offers meditation to their clients.

2. It is practical and something we can do alone, unlike going to church or therapy.

3. Meditation now receives widespread media coverage. Sports trainers and health care professionals openly advocate meditation; editors and advertisers portray meditation as a normal part of everyday life.

4. Popular culture now includes meditation. Although first developed in India 7000 years ago and introduced to ancient Greece nearly 3,000 years ago, a large part of this contemplative knowledge was lost over time. Five centuries ago, European intellectuals explored Asian mystical philosophies, with roots in meditation, as a by-product of the vast world wide exploration of the time. The 20th century emerged with a re-introduction to meditation. But it took the revolution in thinking of the 1960s generation—and events like the Beatles learning meditation— to create widespread public awareness of the practice. As the 'flower power' generation enters middle age, many of their youthful values gain broad-based acceptance. 'Normal' for many people now means: to question religious dogma, act out of concern for the environment or use natural therapies to heal ourselves.

> Meditation is a straightforward way to explore our own, personal spirituality.

5. In recent years we have gained access to vast reservoirs of knowledge from a world of cultures. We choose from the best of an array of traditions. When asked why I choose a spiritual practice originating from a foreign culture, I reply that just because something originates in another country does not mean it is unsuitable. No one believes that computers, first developed in America, are not useful everywhere.

Meditation originated in India, has millennia of acceptance in Asia, but people from all backgrounds directly experience its benefits.

6. Meditation is a straightforward way to explore our own, personal spirituality. While institutionalized religion has recently disillusioned many people, meditation offers us a method to enter our own inner world to pursue a direct spiritual experience.

Meditation is a Practice

Although we hear the praises of meditation in a hundred languages, it is surprising how few people actually meditate. Many people think meditation is a good thing, and tell themselves (or me) that they intend to 'try it one day.' People tell me that they believe in meditation but they don't actually do it. This is like saying 'I believe in swimming' without ever taking the first stroke. We cannot experience the benefits of meditation by reading about it, hearing about it, or philosophizing, or listening to music by some rock star who used to meditate, any more than we can learn to swim from a book. A swimmer has to jump in and get wet. If we want to understand meditation, we have to practice.

Although reading about meditation is no substitute for practicing, it is important to understand the basics of meditation and its purpose. In spite of the great amount of information available, there is still some confusion!

Today a common reason to practice meditation is relief from stress. But relaxation is not the main purpose of meditation—it is just a wonderful side effect. This book focuses on what the Sages of old felt to be the main purpose of meditation: discovery of one's 'Inner Self.' These Sages developed methods of meditation at a time when relaxation and stress management were not the primary concerns of humankind. Meditation has its roots in the knowledge propagated by Sages living in ancient India. It evolved as a response to the human yearning to know the Inner Self—to know the mystical spiritual world, which we may sometimes glimpse but seldom truly grasp. Far more than just a therapy, it can bring spiritual fulfilment to a level beyond ordinary understanding. Who can comprehend the Enlightenment of the Buddha, or the ecstasy of the saints and Yogis? These experiences take us far beyond ordinary thinking...yet merely by virtue of being human we all possess the potential to attain ever-higher spiritual states.

> ...those who choose to walk the path of Self-Realization discover an inner world of love, bliss and wisdom beyond imagining. How much better to radiate love rather than merely reflect it!

People tend to shy away from actively pursuing enlightenment for themselves. After all, it looks like a lot of work and it appears to be awfully difficult to actually attain enlightenment—or to even understand what that means. In the past, most people instead elected to worship those illuminated saints and yogis, but not to practice meditation themselves. Yet those who choose to walk the path of Self-Realization discover an inner world of love, bliss and wisdom beyond imagining. How much better to radiate love rather than merely reflect it!

Meditation Leads to Self Knowledge

When I was in Nepal in 1979 undergoing my training as a meditation teacher, we sat for meditation six hours each day. My mind became so clear and my concentration so sharp that I found that I could easily discern the inner meaning of difficult philosophy books. It was as if I already knew the information intuitively. If we want to understand spiritual concepts, it is best to first practice meditation to develop our intuition rather than just studying intellectual ideas. If we first understand ourselves through meditation, we will more easily understand everything else.

> *"If you want to know all, know One, and that One is your own Inner 'I.'"*
>
> Shrii Shrii Anandamurti

Spiritual understanding is not an intellectual process. It comes from inner knowledge and self-realization. Some saints—such as Sri Ramakrishna—were illiterate, yet they developed a deeper understanding of the ultimate truth than the greatest intellectuals or scholars. That is why this book is not about philosophy, health or relaxation. It is purely about meditation practice—the key to higher awareness.

Why I Wrote this Book

In Close Your Eyes & Open Your Mind I aim to explain meditation in a simple way, without losing sight of its deeper spiritual purpose. Wonderful books have been written about meditation, yet I have not found one that teaches what I have learned, and many of them are quite difficult to understand. Although this book is for general consumption, I originally wrote it for my University students. As I was in University myself when I learned meditation, I am especially passionate about showing students the value of meditation.

Here's what you will find inside 'Close Your Eyes & Open Your Mind:'

1. Questions addresses commonly asked questions, helps to remove doubts or confusion, and explains what you might get out of a regular meditation practice.

2. Donkey Maintenance reveals secrets used by Yogis for thousands of years to keep their bodies healthy and strong for their meditation practice.

3. Close Your Eyes clarifies the first step of meditation—calming the mind and turning attention towards our inner Self.

4. Concentration describes focus, and what it means to be in the present moment.

5. Mantra: The Song of the Inner World explains auditory science and the role of sound and words to elevate our state of consciousness.

6. Open Your Mind: Ego and Intuition explores different levels of consciousness and demonstrates the importance of our attitude in determining our life's direction.

7. Karma: Be Yourself—Everyone Else is Taken casts light on this often misunderstood concept, and illustrates how our actions affect our state of mind.

8. Open Your Eyes discusses how we can apply our insights through meditation, for the benefit of society and the world.

There are different kinds of spiritual meditation coming from a variety of traditions. I have not practiced them all since it can take a lifetime to become adept in just one technique. But I do not believe that this is a problem. If we are in a dry land and need to dig for water, just one hole is enough. But we must go deep. Digging many shallow holes will not quench our thirst. The principles described here can be applied to any kind of meditation. The spiritual nature of human beings is universal, and the human mind has the same intrinsic characteristics the world over. I believe regularity of practice is more important than any particular style practiced. If we learn an effective technique and apply it sincerely, this is the way to satisfy our spiritual thirst.

> If we are in a dry land and need to dig for water, just one hole is enough. But we must go deep.

Although this book is intended as a practical introduction to meditation, it is important to remember that no book is a substitute for a good teacher. If you desire personal instruction in meditation, I encourage you to find a spiritual teacher.

I've included addresses and websites in the appendix to assist you in this search.

Meditation brings about a change for the better on all levels: emotional, physical, mental and spiritual. When I think of the way I

> Our meditation benefits not only ourselves-our efforts create ripples touching those around us and spreading outwards across the universe... forever.

have changed as a result of practicing meditation, and of the way millions of others around the world have changed as well, I am filled with a great hope. It is clear: humanity needs a new vision.

We need to change ourselves from the inside out—and clearly there is a way to do it. Our meditation benefits not only ourselves—our efforts create ripples touching those around us and spreading outwards across the universe...forever. And as people change, the world also changes. It is my hope that this book will guide you on your inner journey as you walk the upward leading path that finally we all must walk.

Dada Nabhaniilananda

"When we become interested in meditation, it is a sign that we are ready to take the journey to another level. As long as the journey remains an outer one, the real goal of our endeavours is never in sight. We continue looking out there for our destination, never realising that the 'I' that is doing the looking is what we are actually looking for."
Chuang-Tse

Chapter One

Questions

"The important thing is to not stop questioning. Curiosity has its own reason for existing. One cannot help but be in awe when we contemplate the mysteries of eternity, of life, of the marvellous structure of reality. It is enough if we try merely to comprehend a little of this mystery every day. Never lose a holy curiosity."
Albert Einstein

When we close our eyes and enter the private realm of our own minds, we find ourselves in another world. Here everything is different. Thoughts behave differently than things. True, experiences, images and memories arise from the outside world, but feelings, sensations, ideas and understanding originate within us. These interact with our outer impressions of the outside world to create an internal universe with a unique terrain, governed by its own laws and seemingly endless possibilities.

Long ago, yearning to uncover the mysteries of this inner self, Yogis developed the practice of meditation. Through the mastery of this practice, it is possible to understand oneself more deeply. But it can go further than that. Through meditation we can gain control over our minds, transform ourselves and realize our true potential.

> Through meditation we can gain control over our minds, transform ourselves and realize our true potential.

This book explains how meditation works, and how to practice it. We begin by addressing a few commonly asked questions.

1. So what exactly is meditation?

Meditation has been defined as a kind of concentrated thinking, but this does not mean just any kind of concentrated thinking. Concentrating on a pet rock or ice cream is not meditation. Meditation is the process of concentrating the mind on the source of consciousness within us. Gradually this leads us to discover the infinity of our own consciousness. This is why the goal of meditation is often described as 'Self-Realization.'

2. What is spirituality?

"Spirituality is that which concerns Infinite Consciousness."

Let me make it clear that 'spirituality' should not be confused with 'spiritualism,' which involves itself with mediums, psychics or communicating with the dead. Spirituality concerns Infinite Consciousness—the same Ultimate Truth as realized by the great spiritual teachers throughout history, such as Buddha, Jesus and Krishna. Spiritual philosophy espouses that the goal of life is to merge the individual mind into Infinite Consciousness; the way to attain this is through the practice of spiritual meditation.

3. What is Self Realization?

The goal of meditation is to realize who we really are at the core of our being. Yoga philosophy describes two distinct levels to our inner self: mental (which includes emotional) and spiritual.

The mental self is sometimes called the individual mind. It is limited because it is strongly associated with our limited physical body and is the cause of the feeling 'I am this individual person.' This is our ego speaking.

Yet our sense of self-awareness comes from our connection to a more universal, subtle form of consciousness. Yogic philosophy describes a reflection of an infinite, all-knowing form of consciousness within our minds. This Infinite Consciousness is unchanging and eternal; it is at the core of our true spiritual 'Self.'

> Infinite Consciousness is unchanging and eternal; it is at the core of our true spiritual 'Self.'

Identification with the small, ego-centered self is called Relative Reality, because that 'small self' is prone to change and death. When we realize the subtler, permanent reality behind the Relative one and we see that our true nature is pure unlimited Consciousness, this is known as Self Realization.

4. What is the difference between meditation and Yoga?

A common understanding of Yoga is as a series of physical exercises that stretch and tie our bodies into impossible knots. But these physical postures are only one aspect of yoga, known as 'Asanas.' The physical postures of yoga are practiced for their health benefits and because they help to prepare the body for meditation. Yoga is both a philosophy of life and a system of spiritual practice. The word 'yoga' actually means union between the individual self and Infinite Consciousness. Meditation is the most important practice in the yoga system and is the means by which this merger or union is achieved. So yoga is a system or science that enables an individual to develop themselves physically, mentally and spiritually. Meditation is the practice that makes the mental and spiritual development possible.

5. I've tried meditation but I can't stop thinking. Am I doing it wrong?

The idea that you have to stop thinking in order to meditate is misleading. It is true that in the highest spiritual states normal thinking modes are suspended, but for most people this is a long way off. And, the way to achieve this state is not by trying to stop thought. You can meditate quite successfully by developing your concentration through regular practice. Do not try to think of 'nothing' or try to stop the thought process. This will only frustrate you. The mind needs something to focus on. This is where the Mantra comes in. Just focus on mentally repeating your Mantra. When other thoughts or feelings distract you, as soon as you become aware of that, simply direct your attention back to the Mantra. Then if your mind wanders again, as soon as you notice that, just direct your attention back to the Mantra again. It's a bit like training a dog: it takes repetition and patience.

> Do not try to think of 'nothing' or try to stop the thought process. This will only frustrate you. The mind needs something to focus on.

You will learn about Mantra meditation in Chapter Five.

6. Is meditation a science?

Science (from Latin scientia – knowledge) is most commonly defined as the investigation or study of nature through observation and reasoning, aimed at finding out the truth. The term science also refers to the organized body of knowledge humans have gained by such research.

Since the Yogic approach to spirituality uses both observation and reasoning to get at the inner truth, and there is an extensive body of knowledge associated with the tradition of Yoga, it can technically be referred to as a science, though some prefer the term 'rational spirituality.'

Meditation has also been described as 'Intuitional Science.' Extensive laboratory tests demonstrate the physiological effects of meditation, but this only shows us its physically measurable effects. Even a recording of a person's brainwave patterns is just a measurement of physical electrical waves. It does not tell us exactly what they are thinking or feeling. The only real laboratory for testing meditation is the mind itself, and the results need to be experienced personally. 'Tantra' is another name for this science, the discipline of spiritual meditation, which enables the practitioner to merge his or her individual mind into Infinite Consciousness.

7. Can Spirituality reconcile with Scientific Rationality?

The central idea of spirituality—that Infinite Consciousness is the ultimate reality—is common to most Asian and some Occidental forms of mysticism. It is not so remarkable that this idea is widely accepted by mystics and philosophers. And in the last century many scientists delineated parallels between quantum theory and the mystical view of reality as described in the ancient texts of Taoism, Buddhism and Yoga. Albert Einstein and virtually all his contemporaries including Niels Bohr, Erwin Schrodinger and Max Planck (in fact most of the pioneers of modern physics) testified to a belief in mysticism. When Werner Heisenberg, discoverer

> many scientists delineated parallels between quantum theory and the mystical view of reality as described in the ancient texts of Taoism, Buddhism and Yoga.

of the Heisenberg Uncertainty Principle, went to India and met with Rabindranath Tagore, the Nobel prize winning poet and great Yogi, he was enormously relieved to find someone who didn't think his ideas were crazy. The ancient yoga philosophy seemed to be saying much the same thing about Reality as the emerging Quantum Theory. This topic, though fascinating and the subject of much discourse, particularly since the 1960s, is beyond the scope of this book. If you want to learn more about this subject I recommend two books: The Tao of Physics by Fritjov Capra, and The Unity Principle by Steven Richheimer.

8. What is mysticism?

"The unending endeavour to bridge the gap between the finite and the infinite is mysticism."

Shrii Shrii Anandamurti

"The most beautiful and most profound emotion we can experience is the sensation of the mystical. It is at the root of all true science. Someone to whom this emotion is a stranger, who can no longer stand rapt in awe, is as good as dead. That deeply emotional conviction of the presence of a superior reasoning power, which is revealed in the incomprehensible universe, is my idea of God."

Albert Einstein

9. What is the difference between Spirituality and Religion?

Founders of the great religions all taught spirituality, yet religion and spirituality are not the same thing. When my own spiritual master was asked if he was trying to start a new religion he replied:

"I am not interested in religion. I am interested in human beings and the goal of human beings, and how to bridge the gap between the two."

within all major religions there are mystical traditions that include many of the features of spirituality.

Many religions may make the same claim, but the reality is that all too often the spirituality taught by the founder gets lost or obscured by dogma and ritual. Notice the profound differences between the catechism of Christ and the practices of mainstream Christianity; between what Krishna taught and Hinduism; and between the teachings of the Buddha and Buddhism as practiced today. Over time, divisions develop within religions, leading to conflict, persecution and even war. When you look at the darkest periods of religious history, it is hard to believe that people could depart so far from the exalted teachings of their great founders. The original message may have been 'spiritual,' but that Spirit gets diluted or lost through a variety of processes: mistranslation and misinterpretation; the loss of spiritual meditation practice; attempts to cloak spiritual concepts in dogma for personal gain; and when religions become religious-political institutions.

Many religions espouse irrational dogmas that have nothing to do with spirituality. I recall my spiritual master laughing about the Hindu superstition that bathing in the Ganges River washes away all your sins and guarantees you a place in heaven. "If that is true," he said, "then the fish living in that river must be the most spiritually evolved creatures in the world!"

Just because a 'holy' book makes some claim does not necessarily mean it is true. Some scriptures say that women have to re-incarnate as men in order to achieve spiritual salvation. Other texts state that you can only come to God by following (coincidentally enough) that same book. This kind of irrational dogma drives many religions. Our common sense can distinguish between dogmas and genuine spirituality.

Yet within all major religions there are mystical traditions that include many of the features of spirituality. This includes the Sufis, Christian mystics, Yogis and the Essenes. But these mystical practitioners almost invariably represent a small minority who are often branded as heretics and persecuted.

What remains in our various religions is a confusing blend of spiritual truth and dogmatic, narrow, irrational doctrines, proclaimed as truth by religious authorities. If we wish to sift out the spiritual elements, it is important to understand the real differences between spirituality and religious dogma. With the passing of time, these differences within mainstream religion have become increasingly distinct:

a. Spirituality is theistic, supporting a belief in the existence of a personal God as creator and controller of the universe. Bear in mind, this is a highly developed and rational concept of God or Infinite Consciousness. Religious belief can be theistic, as in Judaism, Christianity, Hinduism, Tibetan Buddhism and Islam, or atheistic, as in some forms of Theravada Buddhism and Shintoism. Dogmatic Religions generally have either a poorly developed and irrational concept of God, or no concept of God at all.

b. Spirituality is non-dualistic, and states that the purpose of human life is to merge one's self (or sense of 'I') into Infinite Consciousness. Theistic religions tend to be dualistic, propounding both a fundamental separation between God and the world, and the belief that the purpose of human life is to enter into a relationship with God and go to heaven after one dies.

c. Spirituality is practical, and can be experienced and realized by practicing spiritual meditation. The focus is inward, taking the practitioner towards a personal realization. Religions, on the other hand, emphasize faith and belief. Although they teach people different types of prayer, most of the actual practice is externally focused, involving rituals, festivals and ceremonies.

> Spirituality is a lifestyle choice, integrated into every aspect of a person's existence.

d. Spirituality is a lifestyle choice, integrated into every aspect of a person's existence. Much of Religion is a ritualistic, compartmentalized part of a person's life, practiced primarily in temples and churches.

Religion can only serve its proper purpose of liberating the faithful from ignorance and spiritual darkness, to the degree that it remains true to its original spirituality.

10. What is Spiritual Meditation?

In spiritual meditation our mind is directed towards a spiritual idea. The simplest way to conceptualize this is to think of infinite love, peace and happiness—or of an entity that embodies this. We may call it God but the name is not important. What is important is to remember that this Infinite Love is within us, surrounding us and always with us.

Spiritual meditation is concentration on a spiritual idea, one associated with Infinite Consciousness, the source of our awareness. As we contemplate this vast and beautiful idea, our mind gradually transforms into pure consciousness that has no boundary.

Spiritual meditation: the effort to merge our sense of 'I' into Infinite Consciousness.

11. What is the difference between prayer and meditation?

This depends exactly what you mean by the word 'prayer.' Here is what some contemporary Christian experts say:

"Contemplation, or meditation in some groups, was rediscovered in contemporary times beginning with the writings of Thomas Merton in the 1950s and 1960s. The word most Christians are more familiar with is simply prayer.

"Unfortunately, in the West, prayer had become something functional; something you did to achieve a desired effect—which too often puts the ego back in charge. As soon as you make prayer a way to get what you want, you're not moving into any kind of new state of consciousness. It's the same old consciousness, but now well disguised: 'How can I get God to do what I want God to do?' It's the egocentric self, deciding what it needs, but now, instead of just manipulating everybody else, it tries to manipulate God.

"This is one reason religion is so dangerous and often so delusional. If religion does not transform people at the level of both mind and heart, it ends up giving self-centered people a very pious and untouchable way to be on top and in control. Now God becomes their defense system for their small self! Even Jesus found this to be true of the scribes, Pharisees and teachers of the law."

Adapted from CAC Foundation Set: Gospel Call to Compassionate Action and Contemplative Prayer

I would go further to say that as long as it is based on a dualistic conception of God, meaning that human beings and God are kept inherently separate, prayer cannot be considered spiritual meditation. Spiritual meditation places no limit on our realization. It is a non-dualistic practice, and its goal is to merge our inner 'I' feeling with the Infinite Consciousness.

> Philosophically, praying to God to request some thing or action, even for someone else, is illogical.

Evidence of the existence of religion dates back more than 40,000 years. Early religions were animistic, believing that the forces of nature were beings or Gods, and later pantheistic, worshiping many deities and assigning divinity to the invisible but powerful forces of nature that held sway over people's lives. These fearsome gods were appeased through prayer or sacrifice. As society evolved, people gradually realized that there must be a single guiding power behind all these forces of nature, and theism—the belief in only one God—emerged. But the relationship was still based on fear, flattery, appeasement and attempts to persuade God to grant special favors to individuals. Some religious prayer makes that attempt to this day.

Philosophically, praying to God to request some thing or action, even for someone else, is illogical. All the theistic scriptures of the world believe that God is an all-knowing (omniscient), infinitely benevolent being ('God is love'), who already knows if somebody's mother is sick or someone is unhappy, and by logical extension definitely cares enough to do whatever is necessary to help them. Any concerns, or ideas we have originate with God anyway, so telling God how to run the universe seems inappropriate, to say the least.

Yoga philosophy affirms that since Infinite Consciousness gives us everything, we need not ask that Entity for anything. But if we insist on asking for something, we should ask only for more love for God. This is known as devotion.

Prayer takes various forms. Intercessory Prayer is asking for God's intervention in our affairs. More developed forms of prayer include prayers of gratitude, worshipful prayer, contemplative prayer and meditative prayer. These help bring the worshipper closer to God through cultivation of devotion and the feeling of attraction towards Infinite Consciousness.

I believe that all of the great spiritual teachers practiced some kind of spiritual meditation and initiated their closest disciples into this practice. This was their treasured 'inner teaching.' With the passing of time, however, this esoteric portion of their teachings was lost or watered down, and subsequent followers received only the more superficial teachings about morality and philosophy. What is the key to realizing what these enlightened individuals attained? Spiritual meditation! Some subtle forms of contemplative prayer could also be described as spiritual meditation.

11. Do you have to be a monk to be successful in meditation?

Clearly not. Buddha was a monk, but Shiva—regarded by many as the father of yoga— had three wives. (This was not unusual 7,000 years ago). Swami Vivekananda was a monk; my own Guru, ShriI Shrii Anandamurti, was married. And many great spiritualists were women, such as St Theresa of Avila, who was a nun and Anandamayi Ma, who was married.

I chose to be a monk for both personal and practical reasons. This choice should not be viewed as any kind of pre-requisite for spiritual practice or success on the spiritual path.

12. Isn't it self-centered to sit around meditating all the time when there is so much suffering in the world?

It rather depends on what you would be doing if you weren't meditating. If the answer is 'watching television,' by all means, meditate. But if it means you are neglecting your family or using it as an excuse to avoid doing something for others, that is another matter.
Find more details about this subject in Chapter Seven.

13. Is meditation a form of brainwashing?

While surely it is true that the minds of some people would benefit with a good wash, I have to say that meditation is not a form of brainwashing. Usually when people express concern about brainwashing, they are afraid of losing control of their minds and being manipulated.

Meditation actually helps to protect us against having our minds manipulated, by strengthening our willpower and making us more self-aware.

If you're seriously concerned about other people manipulating your mind for their own purposes, I suggest that the first thing you do is switch off your television, a device which is used to great effect by corporations and politicians seeking to influence the behaviour of their audience.

> If you're seriously concerned about other people manipulating your mind for their own purposes, I suggest that the first thing you do is switch off your television

14. Where did the practice of meditation first develop?

Tantric meditation was first developed by the tribes of South India 10,000 - 15,000 years ago, as an expression of their natural desire to understand their own consciousness. About 7,000 years ago it was further developed by Shiva, the great Yogi of ancient India. This practice has since spread and been absorbed into different mystical traditions, including yoga, Taoism, Sufism, Zen Buddhism and Tibetan Buddhism. Similar practices also emerged in indigenous cultures.

15. When did meditation come to the West?

Meditation practices were introduced into Europe at the time of the ancient Greeks, some of who travelled to the East and learned from Indian Yogis and philosophers. Alexander the Great, a student of Aristotle, brought a Yogi back with him from India to be his spiritual advisor. The great Greek mystic and social reformer, Apollonius, found wisdom in the East and was greatly revered for his spiritual power. An advocate of universal religion, he propagated the idea of internal—rather than external—worship. Refusing to champion one popular cult against another, he declared that he 'was concerned with the spirit rather than the form of religion.'

> A most refined celebration of this merging of cultures is expressed in the writings of the great Indian mystic and philosopher Shrii Shrii Anandamurti

The early Judaic and ancient Egyptian religions were heavily influenced by Asian mysticism. Many people believe that Jesus practiced and taught a form of Yogic meditation that he learned in India during the 18 years of his life that are not chronicled in the Bible.

After the collapse of the western half of the Roman Empire in the fourth century, when most of the libraries of Europe were burned, Yogic meditation practices died out in the West. Later, both indigenous and Christian mysticism faced actively suppression, particularly during the dark period of the Inquisition. Europe became a spiritual desert, focusing its attention on intellectual and technological development, militarism, trade, exploration and conquest. Religious institutions started to take a greater interest in politics than in spirituality.

In the mid-nineteenth Century a spiritual renaissance began in Western civilization, spearheaded by such transcendentalist thinkers as Ralph Waldo Emerson and David Thoreau, and through the reintroduction of Asian meditation practices by Swami Vivekananda, the dearest disciple of the great Indian saint, Sri Ramakrishna. Vivekananda was the first modern Yogic master to come to the West, at the beginning of the twentieth Century. This period saw the emergence of the Theosophists, Rudolf Steiner's School of Anthroposophy and a growing interest in Eastern mysticism among European intellectuals like Carl Jung, Aldous Huxley and Herman Hesse. Other Eastern teachers followed Swami Vivekananda, and the 1960s fostered an explosion of interest in Eastern spirituality in Europe and America that quickly spread across the globe—even as far as New Zealand.

A most refined celebration of this merging of cultures is expressed in the writings of the great Indian mystic and philosopher Shrii Shrii Anandamurti (1922 – 1990) who was the first spiritual teacher to develop a full-fledged and harmonious blending of Western rationality and Eastern mysticism. He was the founder of the modern spiritual movement, Ananda Marga, meaning 'The Path of Bliss.' (If you want to know more about his life and teachings I strongly recommend the biography, Anandamurti—The Jamalpur Years by Devashish Acosta.)

Although spiritual meditation originated in southern India in ancient times, its influence can be found in many spiritual traditions. Today it continues to address the universal human need for self-understanding and spiritual fulfilment.

16. What kind of meditation do you teach?

I teach a form of Tantric meditation through the modern yoga and meditation school, Ananda Marga.

The nature of the object or idea you choose to concentrate on in meditation dictates the outcome. Meditation can be done for spiritual growth, for relaxation and stress reduction, or even for some other reason such as success in a sport or a career. The distinguishing feature of all spiritual meditation techniques, as taught in the great spiritual traditions, is that the technique has a single goal: merging with and becoming one with Infinite Consciousness. To put it another way, meditation helps us to realize that we always have been one with infinite Consciousness.

In Tantric meditation, the practitioner learns, through a process of initiation, a personal technique and Mantra (which is repeated mentally). He or she is taught how to withdraw the mind from the external world and concentrate internally. The primary goal of Tantric meditation is to merge one's individual consciousness into Infinite Consciousness. This

> The nature of the object or idea you choose to concentrate on in meditation dictates the outcome.

is the meditation taught by myself and other teachers in the modern Tantric school of Ananda Marga.

17. You only practice one type of meditation- how can you be objective about other methods?

Only an enlightened soul is perfectly objective. The technique I am practicing is the best I have found. Otherwise I'd be doing something else. I try to keep an open mind, and from my study of a wide variety of teachings I understand that there are common psychological and spiritual principles used in spiritual practice. The extent to which these principles are understood and applied determines the effectiveness of a technique in taking us forward on the path of spiritual progress.

For example, it is a widely accepted tenet of psychology that 'as you think, so you become.' When this principle is applied to spiritual meditation, it means we should concentrate on the idea of Infinite Consciousness in order to become serene, loving and God-conscious. But if we have been taught since childhood to feel guilty, or afraid of God, this makes it more difficult to practice. If, on the other hand, we are taught that we are children of the Divine, and that our true nature is perfect and loving, then the feeling of bliss in meditation comes far more naturally.

It is not necessary to learn all techniques in order to grasp how they work...which is fortunate as this is an impossible task for just one lifetime!

18. How do I know if this is the right meditation technique for me?

Some things you must decide for yourself. If you come across a practice that makes sense to you, I suggest you try it. If you then experience that it is bringing the kind of changes you desire, keep doing it. If you experience difficulties, be patient. Don't hastily switch to another technique. You may face the same problem again—and then be forced to realize that the problem may be with you and not with the technique. If, after giving it your best shot, it still doesn't seem to be working, try something else. But don't keep shopping around forever— you should try to find a technique you're happy with and commit to it. Remember those holes we were digging for water? If you keep starting new holes you're going to end up very thirsty.

19. Do I need to have a Guru to learn meditation?

The word 'Guru' means 'dispeller of darkness, and really refers to the Infinite Consciousness acting as a spiritual teacher and guide to individual souls. Since Infinite Consciousness is omnipresent, the real Guru is within us already.

> the real Guru is within us already.

When an individual has attained Self Realization, they are often referred to as a Guru, because the Infinite Consciousness within them is able to act and speak without the distortions of ego. They are then in a position to play the role of a perfect spiritual teacher and guide to others.

In the Bhagavad Giita, Arjuna asked his Guru, Krishna, whether it was possible to attain enlightenment through the guidance of the Divine, Inner Guru, without the assistance of a Guru in physical form. Krishna told him that while it is not essential to have a physical Guru, it will probably take you about 10,000 times as long to attain enlightenment.

Thirty years ago, I wanted to learn meditation but I didn't know how to begin. I read some books on the subject, and with what wisdom I could glean from their pages I began to practice. Which means I wasn't teaching myself—I was learning from various authors. Indirectly, they were my first— in some cases deceased—teachers. Soon I realized that I desired clearer guidance and I began searching for a living teacher or Guru.

> When we are entering the mysterious realm of consciousness, the most rational course is to take the advice of a guide who knows the territory well.

The fact that you're reading this book indicates that you want information about meditation. All of the knowledge in this book comes, directly or indirectly, from a Guru. Literally all of the spiritual books of the world derive their ideas from great spiritual teachers—Gurus. Gurus are the pioneers on the spiritual path who go before us and light the way to guide those who follow.

Some people fear that having a Guru means you must follow blindly. This is a misconception. My Guru, Shrii Shrii Anandamurtii, often quoted an old scripture that says that if a child says something rational we should accept it, and if God Himself says something irrational we should discard it like a straw. Genuine spirituality acknowledges rationality.

And what is the rational course when seeking self-knowledge? When we are entering the mysterious realm of consciousness, the most rational course is to take the advice of a guide who knows the territory well.

This territory can often be quite deceptive and difficult to traverse. If you read about the lives of great mystics like St Francis of Assisi or Milarepa of Tibet, you see that they all faced many trials and tests to transcend the temptations of pleasure and power in order to attain true greatness. At these higher stages on the spiritual path, the guidance of the Guru is even more important.

If you do not have the chance to meet personally with a real Guru (as they are few and far between), do not despair. It is possible to learn from a Guru through their writings, through learning of their inspiring example, and directly from people they appointed to pass on their teachings and techniques. Through meditation, it is possible to establish a personal relationship with your own inner Guru.

20. What does meditation cost?

Traditionally spiritual meditation is taught free of charge and is available to all regardless of a person's economic status. Meditation is a subtle spiritual practice and to attach monetary value to it taints and degrades this spiritual gift.

Nevertheless, there is a personal price. To get results from meditation, you have to put something into it—your own valuable time and effort.

21. How much time does it take?

I recommend that beginners spend at least 15 minutes twice a day in meditation. Later increase to two half-hour sessions. This should bring good results, though some people choose to meditate for longer periods and experience even greater benefit. How much you get out of your meditation is directly related to what you put into it.

22. What benefits have you experienced as a result of meditation?

The benefits I experience personally from this practice include:

a. More mental peace.

b. More emotional balance. I am a musician—this is a very real benefit for someone with an artistic temperament!

c. More creativity. I have always practiced a variety of creative arts, and when I started meditation I felt that I'd tapped into a rich new spring of inspiration, ideas and insights. Many writers, musicians and thinkers report that their inspiration usually comes when the mind is quiet. It seems quite natural that the calming effect of meditation gives us easier access to the deeper, creative level of our minds.

d. A profound sense of purpose in life. I have a growing sense that all life is moving in a positive direction—towards greater awareness, towards a greater feeling of Oneness and harmony. I feel that I am also a part of that same flow of conscious evolution.

e. Improved self-awareness. Introspective practice makes us more aware of our own motivations and qualities. While not always comfortable, how can we improve if we don't see ourselves as we really are? More often it is inspiring to discover the amazing potential within ourselves.

f. A developing sense of universal love. As I am more in touch with the source of my own consciousness, I am more aware of the consciousness in everything. I feel more love within my self, and greater love and compassion for others. This naturally helps me relate to others more easily.

g. Improved good health. I lead a very busy life; I travel frequently with constant demands on my time. Yet I do not suffer from stress-related illnesses that afflict many busy people. Meditation and the consequential natural lifestyle are definitely a recipe for a long and healthy life.

h. Improved will power and concentration. Over the years I notice

> I'm more emotionally balanced, more creative, I'm developing as a person, I sense a profound meaning in my life, I feel closer to God, closer to people, I feel more love. Of course I'm happier. I'd have to be crazy not to be!

my mind becoming clearer and stronger. If we exercise a physical muscle, it develops. The same is true of the mind.

i. Looking forward to my time in meditation. Sometimes it is hard work requiring concentration, but when it really flows this experience can be intensely blissful—more blissful than anything else I've experienced. It is far better than taking drugs (or so I'm told).

j. Feeling happier. I am much happier before I started on this path, and this feeling has grown over the years. I'm more emotionally balanced, more creative, I'm developing as a person, I sense a profound meaning in my life, I feel closer to God, closer to people, I feel more love. Of course I'm happier. I'd have to be crazy not to be!

23. How soon will I feel something in my meditation?

This is personal to everyone, however, here's what happened to a friend of mine.

In the early 1970s, Steve, a young man living in Auckland, New Zealand, and his friends became interested in meditation, and they all learned from a Yogi, an Acharya of Ananda Marga like myself. After learning meditation, Steve practiced very regularly, for thirty minutes twice a day but he didn't feel any effect. After a week or two he began to worry and asked his teacher what was wrong. They discussed what he was doing, and the teacher reassured him that he just needed to be patient and keep practicing.

> when he thought nothing was happening during his meditation—were actually an essential part of the process.

Meanwhile, all Steve's friends were enjoying their meditation, and some were having nice experiences. He continued. After another two weeks he became really frustrated and came to his teacher again and said he was not sure if he could go on. The teacher told him, "We are having a weekend meditation retreat in two weeks time. I am sure that if you keep practicing and come to the retreat, something will happen."

Reluctantly Steve agreed to keep trying. He was afraid that if he gave up, his friends would ridicule him, so he kept at it but began to hate meditation. When time for the retreat came around he didn't even want to go, but since he had said he would, he couldn't easily back out without looking like a failure.

The retreat was on Waiheke Island, and everyone had planned to meet at the ferry in the morning. It so happened that Steve's house was infested with wood eating insects called Bora. Since he was going away, he planned to ignite a 'Bora Bomb.' This canister of poisonous gas kills these insects and stops them from eating all the wood; otherwise they will eventually weaken the wood and make the house inhabitable.

So he put his luggage outside, lit the 'Bora Bomb,' came out and locked the door. When he got to the bus stop he realized he had forgotten his wallet. Part of him thought, "Great! Now I'll miss the bus and I'll miss the ferry and I won't have to go to the retreat." But he thought he still had to try to get there in case his friends interrogated him, so he ran home. Then he had to wait for his breathing to slow, as the house was full of poisonous gas. By the time he had caught his breath, went inside holding his breath, retrieved his wallet, and got back to the bus stop, the bus had left.

"Good", he thought, "but I suppose I should try to hitch hike." He was confident that no one would stop to pick him up, as he had tried before and never succeeded in getting a ride from this stop. So he put out his thumb. The first car stopped.

"Where are you going?" the driver asked.

"To the ferry."

"No problem, I'm going there too."

He was caught.

He arrived at the ferry just in time to meet his friends and then he was stuck on the island for a weekend meditating and chanting and eating vegetarian food, all of which he was now beginning to detest. His meditation was worse than ever and he was completely depressed. Everyone else was so happy and high and he thought maybe he was the only person in the world who could not meditate.

If they had not been on an island he would have left and gone home. Finally the last meditation session of the retreat began, and he thought, "This is the last time I am going to meditate in my whole life. Fantastic!" They were all chanting so happily and he was thinking, "So what? Who cares? I just want to get out of here."

He sat down for what he thought would be the last meditation of his life. Within seconds after closing his eyes he had an amazing experience. He felt as if the top of his head had been removed and was open to the whole universe. He lost all awareness of his body and became lost in a blissful trance. Afterwards he felt overwhelmed and went up to people in tears saying, "It works, it works," like a fool. So that wasn't the last time he practiced meditation after all.

A friend calls that my 'can opener story.'

So how soon will we feel something in our meditation? Everyone's mind is different, so it is difficult to answer this question precisely. Some people I know had an incredible experience the first time they sat for meditation. Others find it hard at first, then begin to enjoy it as they develop more concentration and mental stillness. Some, like Steve, have dramatic tales to tell. Others give up and never find out what might have happened if they had persisted just a little longer. One important thing to realize from Steve's story is that all those weeks—when he thought nothing was happening during his meditation—were actually an essential part of the process. A deep change was going on within him all along. It just took some time to surface.

If we really want to know how long we will have to practice meditation before we too can taste its benefits, there is only one way to find out. The sooner we start, the sooner we'll know.

So close your eyes and open your mind, and accept that meditation practice involves some focused time and effort. If you undertake this wonderful practice with sincerity, I am sure you will long thank the day you did.

Try This

•Here are some questions you might ask yourself. I suggest you write down the answers – in fact why not start a meditation journal so you can keep track of your thoughts and realizations as you progress on your journey.

•Your own questions. Try to answer them in as much specific detail as possible:

What do I want out of meditation?
What do I really expect to get out of meditation?
What am I prepared to put into a meditation practice?

"You can chase a butterfly all over the field and never catch it. But if you sit quietly in the grass it will come and sit on your shoulder."
Unknown

Chapter Two

Donkey Maintenance

Donkey Maintenance

Saint Francis of Assisi referred to his body as his 'donkey.' This seems like a fitting metaphor for our body/mind system. The great Indian epic, the Mahabharata (which includes the Bhagavad Giita) uses similar symbolism. Here the chariot and the charioteer represent the body and mind. The horses are our senses and the passenger is the inner witness or the soul (the 'Atman' in Sanskrit).

If we consider the body to be a vehicle for the mind, what does this imply? The experience of driving a well-maintained vehicle in good working order is quite different from that of driving a neglected old wreck on its last legs. Our state of mind is affected by the condition of our body and vice versa. (And if I were a car I would greatly prefer that the driver were not drunk or sleepy.) How clearly can you think when you have a head cold or a fever? And how full of vitality do you feel if you are depressed? When either the body or mind is out of balance, the other also suffers. When the body is in optimum health, we feel better emotionally and think more clearly.

This mind/body connection has been recognized for millennia, but it is only very recently that we have begun to understand how it works in terms of bio-chemistry. Through the research of scientists like cell biologist Dr. Bruce Lipton, (author of The Biology of Belief) we have learned how our moods and thoughts can change our body's chemistry, and amazingly even our DNA. Like it or not, our body and mind are joined in a lifelong dance, every minute of every day. It might be a good idea to keep this relationship harmonious. This is one couple that we really don't want to contemplate divorce.

In light of all this it amazes me that so many people neglect their physical health. Most people take better care of their cars than their

> When either the body or mind is out of balance, the other also suffers. When the body is in optimum health, we feel better emotionally and think more clearly.

bodies. We would not consider filling up our car with dirty gasoline yet we think nothing of putting all kinds of junk food in our own bodies.

A meditator seeking higher awareness needs to how to maintain both body and mind in optimal health. Long ago yogis developed an entire system of health practices designed to do just that. These secrets are found in the traditions of Yoga, Tantra and Ayurvedic medicine.

The Importance of Physical Health for Meditation

> In meditation we train our minds to bring our impulses under control. Eating food, or imbibing substances that cause us to lose control makes this much harder.

For best results in meditation, we need a body that is disease-free and flexible with a balanced flow of energy. This greatly improves our concentration. This involves more than merely not getting ill and being able to sit still and straight. The activity of our nervous system and glandular system directly affect the flow of vital energy (Prana) in our body—and this affects our state of mind. For best results in meditation our nerves, glands and the vital energy system of Chakras need to be in harmony. We cover more about Chakras in Chapter Five. For now you just think of it as maintaining a balanced flow of life energy throughout the body.

In Yoga the physical body is called the Annamaya Kosa, literally the layer of the mind that is composed of food. What we eat and drink influences our state of mind. Everyone knows how eating too much sugar makes young children hyperactive and uncontrollable. Or how even small quantities of alcohol affect our driving performance. In meditation we train our minds to bring our impulses under control. Eating food, or imbibing substances that cause us to lose control makes this much harder.

A Plethora of Advice

These days we find ourselves overwhelmed with information about health, much of it conflicting. Sometimes it seems quasi-religious or is associated with product promotions, so we don't know if the advice is really in our best interests. Sometimes there are contradictions between the words and actions of experts who talk about health but are not healthy themselves. We read of amazing breakthroughs in micro-surgery or gene technology, curing diseases—diseases easily prevented if people simply exercised and ate fewer burgers.

"Every new McDonald's creates 40 jobs. 20 dentists and 20 heart surgeons." - Doucoure on Twitter

"An alcoholic is one who drinks more than his doctor." - Unknown

One 'expert' tells us to eat no protein. Another says eat only protein.

Good cholesterol, bad cholesterol, low-carb diets, hi-carb diets, gluten and lactose intolerance, chemical residues in the food chain, allergies that never existed before, drink gallons of water, drink no water. But wait, no need to worry about any of that. All you have to do is eat this berry from the lost jungles of Brazil and you will live forever!

No wonder people are confused.

I'd like to bring a bit of common sense back into this discussion. Let's start by looking at what is natural for our bodies.

> If everyone followed these few simple guidelines, the health of humanity at large would be transformed.

What is Natural for Humans?

Our physical bodies have not changed significantly during the past 40,000 years. Here's a quick glance at how we humans lived during almost all of our recent past:

• No chairs or computers. The human body is not designed to sit in front of a screen all day. **We need to exercise regularly.**
• We evolved before electricity was invented. **It is more healthy to rise with the sun and sleep during darkness.**
• We evolved before processed food and chemical additives were invented. **Unprocessed food is much more suitable for us.**
• We evolved in a situation of food scarcity and went hungry regularly. **Our bodies are designed to fast periodically.**
• Our anatomy and physiology clearly indicate that we are not designed to eat meat. That is why we have to cook it. **We will be more healthy if we avoid eating meat.**

• Our bodies are composed mostly of water. Water purifies the blood and keeps our internal systems clean. **We should drink plenty of water.**

If everyone followed these few simple guidelines, the health of humanity at large would be transformed.

Incidentally such a shift in behavior would also have huge economic benefits. In the USA the single largest government budget item is health care, and it is growing along with the waistlines of the populace. Most of this enormous health care budget is spent treating preventable, lifestyle-related diseases. If enough Americans followed a more natural, healthier lifestyle, they could simultaneously solve their economic problems.

Disease Prevention vs. Disease Treatment

"First the doctor told me the good news: I was going to have a disease named after me."
      Steve Martin

The modern system of 'allopathic' medicine focuses on disease. We are told as children that germs cause disease. Scientists have made amazing advances in the study of different pathogens and how to kill then when they invade our bodies. Some years ago I was a passenger in a motorcycle accident and suffered abrasions to one foot. I was treated, but a few days later a dark red line crept slowly up my leg, under the skin, so I went back to the hospital. As soon as the doctor saw my leg he almost panicked and put me on an intravenous antibiotic drip. I asked him what would have happened if there were no antibiotics. "We would have had to cut your leg off," he replied. I asked what would have happened if they did not cut my leg off, and he said, "When that red line reached your heart you would have died."

> We didn't expect to find that eating fruit and vegetables would prove to be so important in protecting men against cancer

This gave me a new kind of appreciation of the value of modern medicine in an emergency.

However, most common diseases are more easily prevented or cured using more natural means with fewer side effects.

A report published in the British Journal of Cancer in 2011 said that nearly half of cancers diagnosed in the UK each year—over 130,000 in total—are caused by avoidable life choices including smoking, drinking and eating the wrong things. One of the authors said: "We didn't expect to find that eating fruit and vegetables would prove to be so important in protecting men against cancer. And among women we didn't expect being overweight to be more of a risk factor than alcohol."

More traditional systems of medicine, such as naturopathy, acupuncture and Ayurveda, focus on health rather than on disease. In the old Chinese medical tradition, doctors were paid a regular salary, and if anyone in their community of patients became ill, their pay was reduced. That's an incentive to keep everyone healthy! Nowadays doctors get paid to cure illnesses, so the more people get sick, the more they get paid. And if you think the doctors make money from our illnesses, what about the drug companies! It doesn't seem very smart to reward our medical professionals for treating illness rather than for keeping people healthy.

Yoga teaches us how to better understand our own bodies so that we are not so dependent on doctors and medicines. It is a system of preventative medicine.

> *More traditional systems of medicine, such as naturopathy, acupuncture and Ayurveda, focus on health rather than on disease.*

Digestion

One of the keys to health and longevity is good digestion. Here is something quite simple but very important to understand about digestion:

- Our digestive system has two functions: absorption of nutriments and elimination of toxins.
- Our digestive system cannot perform both of these functions at the same time.
- The primary cause of most common diseases is the build up of toxins in the body. Why? Because toxins weaken our immune system and create a breeding ground for harmful pathogens.
- Eliminating toxins from the body regularly is vital to maintain good health. There are several ways to do this:

• Avoid eating between meals so that our digestive system has a chance to perform its second function of elimination.
• Drink plenty of water.
• Avoid overeating.
• Choose food that is easy to digest so that un-digested food does not decay in our system and create toxic byproducts.
• Undertake periodic fasts.
• Exercise regularly.

Nine Health Secrets of the Yogis

1. Diet
When talking about health, food is the big gorilla in the room, so let's tackle it first. There are a thousand theories and arguments about what we should or should not eat but I do not want to get into a lengthy debate. I prefer to let the ancient wisdom of the yogis take precedence. If we then add a bit of common sense the picture becomes pretty clear. You do not have to be a nutritionist to understand what foods are best for you.

In fact, sometimes having too many advisors just serves to confuse matters. Take the 2011 decision by the US Congress to classify pizza as a vegetable. The big pizza companies wanted to keep selling pizza to schools, but the new health regulations required that more vegetables instead of junk food be served to children. So the corporate lawyers concocted an absurd argument that a school child could see through. The result? Now two tablespoons of tomato sauce supposedly magically converts a slice of white flour dough and some cheese into a vegetable. Don't argue-it is the law.

> Favor alkaline forming foods that are easy to digest.

Sometimes elaborate 'logic' does not serve us as well as common sense. Especially when it is 'corporate logic.'

So don't worry too much about the arguments of hired 'experts.' If you follow the guidelines below as best you can, you'll do substantially better than most people.

a. Favor alkaline forming foods that are easy to digest. This generally means 'lighter' foods, like fruits and vegetables, as opposed to meat and eggs or cheese or sweets. That's right—the stuff that everyone knows is unhealthy is actually unhealthy. Not rocket science is it? And if you eat too much, even of good quality food, it is still bad for you.

b. Prefer sentient food. Yogis are a bit more savvy than most people when it comes to understanding how food affects not just our bodies, but our minds. Here's a simplified list of the preferred diet of yogis, known as 'sentient' or 'sattvic' food.

Sattvic Foods: Good for body and mind—fruits, most vegetables, grains, pulses, beans & milk products.

Rajasic Foods: Not too bad in small quantities—coffee, tea, chocolate, carbonated drinks.

Tamasic Foods: Bad for body or mind—meat, fish, poultry, eggs, onion, mushrooms and garlic. Garlic may have certain health benefits, but it is very agitating for the meditators mind and makes it more difficult to concentrate. (This fact has made a lot of Italian yogis very unhappy...)

Mushrooms are another 'tamasic' item that surprises people. When I first learned meditation I was the kind of student teachers dream of. Whatever my teacher told me I followed strictly without question. When he merely suggested that I follow a Sattvic diet I immediately became a vegetarian and stopped eating onions, mushrooms and garlic. I found this really easy since I didn't like any of those things—with one exception. I was not happy without my mushrooms, so after a couple of months of abstention I thought to myself, "I don't see how mushrooms can be so bad for my meditation. They look pretty harmless to me, and they taste delicious." So I decided to conduct an experiment on myself to see if they really had any bad effect. The next morning I cooked up a plate of fried mushrooms on toast. Delicious! I felt fine and noticed no bad effect, until I sat for meditation that evening. It was terrible. I could not concentrate and my mind felt heavy and dead—no clarity. I learned my lesson and have not eaten mushrooms since.

A lot of people wonder about sugar. While it is not completely proscribed in the yoga diet, it is better to eat little or no sugar, especially as you get older. I gave up refined sugar in 2008 and feel that it was a very good move. As there are plenty of alternative sweeteners such as agave, honey, dried fruit, malt syrup and maple syrup, it is not as if I'm suffering. I'm just far less likely to suffer in the future from hypoglycemia or worse, diabetes.

More on the question of vegetarianism comes later in this chapter. Let's finish with the yogi's health secrets.

2. Proper Exercise

Exercise is of course the second key to vibrant health. It is no secret that if you want to be healthy you should eat less and exercise more. The question is: what kind of exercise and how much?

Yoga recommends two main kinds of exercise:

•Aerobic exercise. The main benefit of this kind of exercise is physical—it maintains fitness and muscle tone. I recommend thirty minutes of strenuous aerobic exercise such as running or swimming, five times a week. Daily would be even better. In addition to this I recommend at least thirty minutes walking a day.

•Vital energy exercises—these are exercises such as yoga or tai chi where the effect is more subtle, creating a harmonious flow of vital energy and relaxation in the body and toning the nerves and glands. This kind of exercise is excellent for stress relief and concentration. It is also very good for preparing the body to sit in meditation. I recommend at least 20 minutes of yoga exercises per day.

> There are two special exercises taught in the Ananda Marga school of yoga which have the benefits of both aerobic and vital energy exercises.

•There are two special exercises taught in the Ananda Marga school of yoga which have the benefits of both aerobic and vital energy exercises. They are yoga dances of Kaoshikii and Tandava. You can learn them in any Ananda Marga yoga center or class.

3. Bathing

Bathing daily obviously keeps our bodies clean. Using cool water, below body temperature, cools the body and calms the mind.

Washing our hands, arms, feet and face with cool water before meditation and before eating has many benefits. It induces a physiological response called the 'diving response' that redirects the blood flow and the body's energy to vital organs, aiding concentration and digestion. Just try washing your feet with cold water after a long walk on a hot day and you will feel immediate relief, not just physically but mentally as well.

4. Drinking water

Water is the elixir of life, and drinking plenty of pure water is one of the greatest of health

> If you are in normal health you should drink 4 - 6 pints (3 - 4 liters) of water every day.

secrets. This helps your body to keep your blood Ph slightly alkaline and gives you more energy, improves digestion and eliminates toxins.

If you are in normal health you should drink 4 - 6 pints (3 - 4 liters) of water every day. This sounds like a lot, but if you space it out between meals it is quite easy. Avoid drinking for 30 minutes before a meal, and for one hour afterwards, otherwise you will dilute your digestive fluids.

5. Fasting

We need to allow our digestive system time to rest so that it is free to eliminate toxins. Our system cannot absorb nutriments and eliminate toxins at the same time, so it is best to avoid eating between meals.

To give our system a longer rest it is good to fast for a whole day. Yogis recommend that we fast for one day, twice a month and fast according to the phases of the moon. Our minds are affected by the moon phases; fasting helps to counteract any negative effect. The eleventh day after full and new moon is known as Ekadashi, a very good time to fast.

Fasting for one day may seem a little daunting at first, but most people find that it is not nearly as difficult as they expected. It is good to break your fast with a system flush. This consists of a large quantity (about 2 pints) of water with lemon and salt. Two flat teaspoons of salt, and half a lemon juiced is just about right. Within about 30 minutes of drinking, this concoction induces a bowl movement that flushes out the toxins your digestive tract has collected for elimination. The feeling afterwards is wonderful—you feel so clean and fresh. Having a clean bowel is great for meditation.

Fasting can also be very helpful in curing disease. If you plan to undertake a longer fast of several days or even weeks, it should be done under supervision. I once did a 21-day juice fast and at the end of it I felt that I'd added years to my life. A doctor conducted tests before and after and confirmed that my liver and kidney functions were completely rejuvenated.

Some years ago I knew a woman in Australia who was diagnosed with liver cancer. She was only thirty years old, and was told she would only live a few months. After she carried out a 30-day, water-only fast, the large tumor in her liver was completely gone. Her doctor was shocked. So how does this happen?

When someone undertakes such intense fast, the body begins to absorb tissue as an energy source after a few days with no food. It is smart enough to target non-essential tissue first. A cancerous tumor is non-essential tissue. This woman's body digested the tumor.

As you can imagine, this type of long fast must be carefully monitored. We don't want our bodies to start digesting more important tissue, like brain cells!

6. Meditation

The immediate cause of many diseases is pathogens—hostile organisms that invade our system. But generally we do not fall prey to these pathogens unless our resistance weakens in some way. Stress is a major factor in weakening our resistance to disease.

Meditation is well known as a stress management method. This is particularly important in our very frazzled modern environment, even as the physiological side effects of meditation practice are well documented.

> Recent studies have shown that people who lead satisfying, meaningful and happy lives also live longer, healthier ones. Which really should be no surprise.

But there is a more subtle and indirect health benefit we get from meditation. Most meditators observe that over time they develop a stronger sense of life purpose and a generally improved feeling of well being. They become happier. Recent studies have shown that people who lead satisfying, meaningful and happy lives also live longer, healthier ones. Which really should be no surprise.

"Always laugh when you can. It is cheap medicine."
Lord Byron

7. Raw Food

Consuming some raw fruits and vegetables every day is another of the secrets of long life. Raw fruits and vegetables contain plenty of fiber and retain important enzymes that are often destroyed by cooking. These enzymes help to digest and absorb the nutrients in food.

A friend in San Francisco helps many people cure diabetes (type 2) and come off insulin, just by convincing them to switch to a raw food for a month. He produced a great video about this, featuring patients accustomed to a diet of hamburgers and Pepsi, testifying to the transformation in their health. Some of them found it difficult at first to adjust to the new diet, but in the end they all felt it was well worth the effort.

8. Yoghurt

Not all bacteria are bad. In fact, most of the various bacteria in our bodies are benign or beneficial. Intestinal bacteria play a vital role in digestion and help to break down food.

The bacteria found in our stomachs are the same that transform milk into yoghurt. To replenish and maintain a healthy population of friendly intestinal bacteria, it is good to take live yoghurt regularly.

9. Proper Rest

Regular, good quality sleep is essential for health. We get the most benefit from sleep between 10 pm and sunrise (assuming you're not in Finland in the summer). This aligns us with the natural cycles of Sun and Earth. Avoid eating before sleeping. Our sleep hinders our digestion—and our digestion disturbs our sleep.

I noticed that when I started to meditate regularly my need for sleep became less. I used to sleep eight hours. Now six hours is plenty. I use the extra time to meditate!

So there you have it: The Nine Yogic Secrets of Long Life. See you on the other side of ninety!

Vegetarianism

"I am not a vegetarian because I love animals.
It is because I hate vegetables."
Woody Allen.

> It is not essential to be a vegetarian in order to meditate successfully.

But before I go into this topic I want to make one thing clear. It is not essential to be a vegetarian in order to meditate successfully. If you are not vegetarian already, treat this section simply as a suggestion.

OK, so here we go.

Why do I, and many other people, prefer a vegetarian diet? I could write a book on this, but I don't need to as several other people have already done an excellent job of that, notably John Robbins in his book Diet for a New America. If you want to understand this issue in depth read his book, or watch the one-hour documentary version. Here's my short version.

There are four good reasons to be vegetarian.

1. I Don't Eat My Friends

"Animals are my friends and I don't eat my friends."
George Bernard Shaw
(winner of the Nobel Prize in Literature 1925)

There is no doubt that by eating meat, we participate in a process that causes a great deal of suffering to animals. As meditators we are naturally cultivating our own sense of compassion. This tends to make us more sensitive to the suffering of others, so avoiding harming animals seems like a natural follow through.

In Diet for a New America, John Robbins tells a story about a nine-year old girl who was sitting with her family at the dinner table one evening. They were eating lamb. They were watching a television program about spring, featuring lambs running about on the grass and playing. At this point the girl suddenly understood that these cute little lambs were what was on her plate. Horrified at what she had been eating, she turned on her parents in tears. "Why didn't you tell me!" she accused them. In her fury, in that moment she declared, "I will never eat meat again. And nor will you!" Such was her moral outrage that the whole family became vegetarian on the spot.

2. A Vegetarian Diet is Healthier

We are not designed to eat meat. Here is a simplified list of physical features of a carnivore, compared to a human:

	Carnivore	Human
Teeth	Sharp teeth for tearing meat	Grinding molars for chewing grains and fruit
Saliva	Acidic	Alkaline
Sweat glands	Have none. Perspire through tongue	Have sweat glands
Digestive tract	Short to digest fast-decaying meat rapidly- three times body length	Long to digest vegetables and fruits - ten times body length

Meat is extremely difficult to digest—that is why we have to cook it and it is at the top of the list when it comes to acid-forming foods. It decays very rapidly because it lacks the rigid cellulose cell wall that supports plant cells. It decays while still in our digestive tract, creating toxic byproducts that pollute our entire system. Eating too much meat is a leading cause of bowel cancer, constipation, rheumatism, arthritis, gout, heart disease and numerous other ailments.

Some insurance companies offer a discount on your health insurance if you're a vegetarian because they know you will cost them less money in medical treatment in the years ahead.

Some insurance companies offer a discount on your health insurance if you're a vegetarian because they know you will cost them less money in medical treatment in the years ahead.

3. Following a Vegetarian Diet Helps our Spiritual Progress

"Until he extends the circle of compassion to all living things, man will not himself find peace."
Albert Schweitzer
(Nobel Peace Prize, 1952)

"Vegetarian food leaves a deep impression on our nature. If the whole world adopts vegetarianism, it can change the destiny of humankind."
Albert Einstein

"My refusing to eat flesh occasioned an inconvenience, and I was frequently chided for my singularity, but, with this lighter repast, I made the greater progress, for greater clearness of head and quicker comprehension."
Benjamin Franklin

"Non-violence leads to the highest ethics, which is the goal of all evolution. Until we stop harming all other living beings, we are still savages."
Thomas Edison

Eating meat has an effect on our minds. Some professional fighters are well aware of this, and are encouraged to eat plenty of red meat leading up to important fights precisely because it makes them more aggressive. Consuming a lot of meat reinforces certain animal instincts in us humans. This is the primary reason yogis avoid eating meat: they are trying to transcend their animal nature through their spiritual practice.

4. It is Better for the Environment

"A 2006 United Nations report identified the world's rapidly growing herds of cattle as the greatest threat to the climate, forests and wildlife. These hordes are the cause of a host of other environmental crimes, from acid rain to the introduction of alien species, from producing deserts to creating dead zones in the oceans, from poisoning rivers and drinking water to destroying coral reefs.

The 400-page report by the Food and Agricultural Organization, entitled Livestock's Long Shadow, also surveys the damage done by sheep, chickens, pigs and goats. But in almost every case, the world's 1.5 billion cattle are most to blame. Livestock—more than cars, planes and all other forms of transport put together—are responsible for 18% of the greenhouse gases that cause global warming".

The Independent - UK 10 DECEMBER 2006

> cultivation of meat as a food source involves extremely inefficient land use. Soybeans produce ten times more protein per acre than cattle.

"Many things made me become a vegetarian, among them the higher food yield as a solution to world hunger."
John Denver

Good point John (and thank you for all the beautiful songs!). This is reason number five: cultivation of meat as a food source involves extremely inefficient land use. Soybeans produce ten times more protein per acre than cattle.

Myths About Eating Meat

Myth 1: "We need meat for protein."

This is nonsensical. Millions of people never eat an ounce of meat in their lives and do not suffer protein deficiency. The thousands of vegetarians I personally know are much healthier than the average person.

With a few exceptions (such as lemons), all foods contain protein. Many vegetarian foods are rich in protein: legumes, seeds, nuts, beans, tofu, cheese, yoghurt and milk. Vegetable protein, unlike meat and eggs, is free of harmful cholesterol. Simply switching from eggs to tofu as a protein source will cause your cholesterol level to plummet.

Myth 2: "We need meat for vitamin B12"

Critically important vitamin B12 is readily available through cheese, whey, yoghurt, milk and yeast extract, to name the top 5 vegetarian sources. None of these come from meat!

Myth 3: "We need 'it' for fatty acids Omega 3, 6, & 9."

Do you believe that only source of these important brain food fatty acids is fish liver oil? This is untrue! Low cost vegetarian sources of omega oils include flax seed, walnuts and hemp.

Myth 4: "Vegetarians are weak and wimpy"

My mum foisted meat on me because she believed it was essential for getting sufficient protein so that I would grow up to be a big strong boy. It's a pity she never read this list of famous athletes who are all vegetarians. Serious non-wimps:

Carl Lewis: 9 Olympic Gold Medals, including 4 in 1984. Feted as "Athlete of the Century"

Martina Navratilova: Tennis player. 18 grand slam singles titles

Robert Parish: Basketball player. Basketball Hall of Fame 2003

Prince Fielder: Baseball player. More than 50 home runs

Dave Scott: Iron Man World Champion—6 times!

Billie Jean King: Tennis player. 12 Grand Slam titles.

Bill Pearl: Bodybuilder. 4 time Mr. Universe.

Joe Namath: American football quarterback. NFL Hall of Fame 1985

And many more...

Here's a quiz question. Who is the least likely celebrity sports champion to become vegetarian? Turn to the end of this chapter to find the identity of the "World's Least Wimpy Vegetarian."

In case you have been told that vegetarianism makes you stupid, here are a few more famous vegetarians:

Albert Einstein
Leonardo Da Vinci
Sir Isaac Newton
Plato
Henry David Thoreau
Pythagoras
Adam Smith
Thomas Edison

George Bernard Shaw
Benjamin Franklin
Paul McCartney
George Harrison
Mahatma Gandhi
Abraham Lincoln
Clint Eastwood
Linda Blair
Bill Clinton

**And a very long list
of other notables.**

Conclusion:

So there you have it if you want it:
the yogi's 'secret' formula for health and
long life.

You may already have adopted some of
these lifestyle choices. Or the whole idea might seem daunting. If you
would like to improve your health by making just a few changes, here
are some suggestions for how you might want to go about it:

A. Take baby steps—don't try to become Superwoman
overnight. Or even Batman.

B. Try some thirty-day trials. Pick just one point to try
for thirty days without committing for longer than
that. If you like it, continue it! Or try something else.

C. Think long term—changes in lifestyle now pay off
hugely when you are older.

D. Remember the compound effect—adopting a small
good habit, repeated daily over time, can bring
  remarkable results. This principle works both ways:
bad habits practiced over a long period result in heavy
attrition.

E. Prioritize. Tackle one thing at a time.

We all have resistance to change. Here are some fun excuses from
the Inner Wimp:

> adopting a small good habit, repeated daily over time, can bring remarkable results. This principle works both ways: bad habits practiced over a long period result in heavy attrition.

•I've been carbo-loading for the last 40 years in case I ever need to go on a 10,000 mile run.

•If God wanted me to touch my toes, he would have put them on my knees.

•I'm on a strict running program. I started yesterday. I've only missed one day so far.

•I get a lot of mental exercise by thinking up weird ways to avoid physical exercise.

"Health Food: any food whose flavor is indistinguishable from that of the package in which it is sold."
   Henry Beard

•We lived for weeks on nothing but food and drink.

•If we're not meant to have midnight snacks, why is there a light in the fridge?

Try This:
Key Recommendations

• Do not eat between meals

• Avoid processed food—eat live food

• Eat less meat or eliminate it (pun intended)

• Drink plenty of water—6 pints a day

• Sleep and rise early

• Exercise (e.g. walk) every day for 45 minutes

• Practice yoga postures daily

• Meditate every day—after all, that's why we're meandering through this book together isn't it?

Write down in your meditation journal any commitments you make to yourself and check on them every week. Or every day!

Quiz question answer:
Mike Tyson, 9-time World Heavyweight boxing champion, became a vegetarian after he won all his titles. He has done quite a bit of soul searching and admits he is not proud of what he had done with his life. He attributes his character reform in part to his vegetarian diet. Is that cool or what?

"I realized meat has become a poison for me now."
Mike Tyson

Chapter Three

Close Your Eyes

"Come away Oh human child
To the waters and the wild
And leave your cares behind...."

W.B. Yeats

The Sufi mystic Mullah Nasruddin had a unique teaching style. One evening a neighbor found the Mullah crawling on his hands and knees under a street lamp outside his house searching for something in the grass.

'What have you lost?' asked the neighbor.

'My keys,' said the Mullah and continued searching.

'Here, let me help you,' said the friendly neighbor. After a short time another neighbor came by and joined the search, and then another, until there was a small crowd of people crawling about in the grass.

Finally the Mullah got up. 'This seems hopeless,' he said.

'Where do you think you lost the keys?' asked the first neighbor.

'In my house,' said the Mullah.

'Then why on earth are we all searching out here under the street lamp?'

'How would we ever find them in the house? It's too dark - you can't see a thing. Out here there is a light!' replied the Mullah.

What the Mullah was doing seems absurd, but it is no more pointless than what most of us do, most of the time, when we expect to find happiness outside of ourselves.

Happiness Comes from Within

"Inside every sad person is a happy person, trying to get out."
Dada Krsnasevananda

It is easy to understand that happiness comes from within our minds. After all, happiness is a mental experience. Yet we associate the experience of happiness so closely with the object that triggers it that we still easily fall into the trap of thinking that the happiness is contained in the object. This can lead to various types of psychological addictions.

> we associate the experience of happiness so closely with the object that triggers it that we still easily fall into the trap of thinking that the happiness is contained in the object. This can lead to various types of psychological addictions.

In India this is how they build a monkey trap: In a coconut shell they make a hole just large enough for the monkey to put its hand inside. They tie the coconut to a tree with some delicious food inside. The monkey smells and searches for the food and puts its hand inside to grab the food. But its clenched fist is too large to come out of the hole. When the hunter approaches, the monkey screams in fear and tries to escape, but its desire for the food is so great that it refuses to let go of the food and unclench its fist in order to escape. He traps himself.

Similarly, our own desires can easily trap us.

But we are no longer monkeys! We humans have greater intelligence, self-awareness and free will. Once we recognise how our own behaviour ensnares us—if we assert our will and control our impulses—we escape from the trap of our own devising. This is a vital step on the path to spiritual freedom.

Easy? Not often. The instinctive side of our nature tempts our minds to run after objects of pleasure or immediate sensory gratification. This pleasure is always temporary—and humans are never satisfied with finite pleasure or happiness. We always want more. We are the only creatures to overeat, overindulge and accumulate ever-increasing wealth and territory, well beyond what we need. Yet even the wealthiest, most powerful kings and dictators don't find satisfaction. There is not enough physical wealth in the entire world to satisfy the yearning of even a single human being.

There is only place to experience the immeasurable happiness of our yearning: the core of our being—infinite consciousness.

The path to happiness lies inward; taking first step on this path requires us to

> if we assert our will and control our impulses—we escape from the trap of our own devising. This is a vital step on the path to spiritual freedom.

withdraw our attention from the external world of the senses.

"In every living being is a thirst for limitlessness."
Shrii Shrii Anandamurti

Meditation begins by leaving our everyday concerns and struggles behind and reaching for something deeper, quieter, and closer to our own personal core. When we sit down to meditate, daily worries and ties to the external world are strong ropes keeping our awareness moored to the docks of our mundane life. They hinder us from embarking to the open waters of our inner being. Start your journey by cutting loose the ropes and casting off the outside world. This first step is 'sensory withdrawal.'

Taking a break

Behind the need to 'break away from it all,' burns an innate desire for that 'something more;' that elusive state that is the basis of our being. Our endeavours and successes in the external world are of course important; they are the physical manifestation of our dreams and aspirations. But when we pin all our hopes on finding happiness or fulfilment 'out there,' disappointment is almost inevitable and we keep looking that missing element.

People invent all sorts of ways to break away and enjoy a little freedom, if only for a few minutes, few hours or days. A weekend camping trip, Hawaii vacations, concerts, parties, a few hours at the local pub or an evening lying in front of the television all easily satisfy our need to get away and leave our burdens behind us (at least for a time).

Love of art and nature encourages more introspection. Music moves us. Attending a concert may transport our mind to some distant place— one that seemed impossibly remote as we sat in the office or behind the wheel of the car, carving our way through endless traffic. Art stirs us. It often takes us to realms inside ourselves that are normally inaccessible; it gives us a glimpse of an interior landscape hidden behind the clouds of our busy lives.

Nature brings a calming influence. The quietness of nature, with its sense of vastness, reflects the colors of the depths inside, like a lake reflecting the brilliance of the sun that resonates with our own limitless Self.

Think for a moment of the collection of things you do to escape. Aren't the majority of them an attempt to connect to the part of our existence that lives deep inside?

"The objects of pleasure do not give us the happiness. The objects are merely keys to the happiness. They momentarily unlock the happiness that is always inside us."
Deshapriya

Sensory Withdrawal

"Try to penetrate as deeply as you can into your mind, keep moving inwards but do not forget the realities of the external world, because if you ignore the external realities, your internal peace will also be disturbed."
Shiva

Our senses connect our mind to the physical world. They are gateways from our inner awareness that receive, perceive and communicate with the reality outside us. Like all gateways, they can be open or shut to regulate access—in this case, to information and experiences. This link, made possible by millions of tiny chemical reactions in the central nervous system, converts physical sensations into impulses carried by nerve cells and fibers. Electro-chemical charges jump with lightning speed across gaps in neuron transmitters/receivers, passing the signals along in both directions. This constant electro-chemical activity keeps the mind connected to the world, enabling us to function.

> The seeker finds refuge from the common life of the senses in a search for self-knowledge.

When we stop the flow of sensory stimuli, we often experience a sense of freedom and peace. Daily stress connects intimately to the flow of information we receive from outside of ourselves. When that connection is broken—even for a short time—we encounter an exhilarating sense of lightness; our burdens suddenly disappear. We feel relief from the tensions associated with the sights, sounds and other stimuli of our environment, as in the old adage 'out of sight, out of mind.' Since the early 1970s psychologists have studied this phenomenon using sensory deprivation experiments. So-called 'samadhi' tanks create an artificial environment to cut subjects off from almost all sensory stimuli. After prolonged periods in these tanks, subjects report profound experiences of joy, tranquillity and freedom from the cares of life.

Human beings have searched for ways to withdraw since the beginning of civilization; it's deeply imbedded in our genetic memory.

During initiation into manhood, young Native American boys traditionally travelled on a vision quest. They withdrew into seclusion in a lonely, isolated place to fast, meditate, ingest herbs and remain awake for several days in an effort to disconnect from their familiar world and enter an inner terrain deeper than themselves. The seeker finds refuge from the common life of the senses in a search for self-knowledge. Not only ascetics and hermits use such methods—this is common in most religious and indigenous traditions in one form or another - we find tales of errant knights fasting all night and praying in the King Arthur stories.

Most of us respond to the need to withdraw from external stimuli instinctively. When we feel a need to get in touch with ourselves, we go off alone to a place where we won't be bombarded by the constant barrage of information that saturates our normal daily life. Often we take refuge in the peace and tranquillity of nature as a simple and effective way to 'slow the traffic' entering through the doors of our senses.

Artificial Methods of Sensory Withdrawal

Another widespread method of putting a temporary halt to our sensory input is through drugs and alcohol. Let's look at what happens when we drink a few glasses of wine to help us relax in the evening after a hard day, or get ourselves good and soused on a Friday night so we can put the week behind us.

Biologically, the alcohol makes the lipid membrane of the nerve cell permeable, thereby deadening the nervous system. When this occurs in cells, the electrical impulse is lost.

Not all the brain cells are destroyed in this process. Many just have holes in them for a few hours. Messages from the world of the senses do not get through, leaving us less and less aware of what is happening outside ourselves. An intoxicated person is far less sensitive to pain while under the influence of alcohol; in fact, one of our common expressions for being intoxicated, 'feeling no pain,' is not just a metaphor. We literally get anesthetized due to the deadening effect of the alcohol. It is a kind of sensory withdrawal. A 'high' is nothing more than a temporary dissociation from the senses. This alcohol-based method of 'taking a break' creates a breach in the pathways of the nervous system, those information highways of the mind. Drugs affect us similiarly. They alter the way that information is passed along nerve fibers, disrupting our normal contact with the world around us.

Once we are disconnected from the world, we find that most of our cares and worries have been left behind (at least for a few hours). We are free to sing out of tune, crazily dance or hug our friends and tell them how much we've always loved them. While some people experience bad reactions from drinking or drugging socially, for many these activities are pleasurable. This is just one more indication that happiness lives within us. By creating this disconnect, alcohol or drugs help us to gain access to some of the happiness and peace within us.

But the effects of these substances are unpredictable. Some people become violent while under the influence. Heavy use of alcohol and drugs wreaks havoc on our body, permanently damages our nervous system, weakens our will power and fosters physiological or psychological dependency. The negative long-term effects far outweigh any transient enjoyment.

The Natural Method of Sensory Withdrawal

While meditation starts with sensory withdrawal, it doesn't deaden the senses (or cause any long-term damage!). Sensory withdrawal is accomplished by quieting the sensory organs and using visualization and mantra to focus the mind so that its connection to the gateways of the senses is suspended. This also strengthens the nervous system and brings it under our control. Unlike artificial methods, there are no harmful side effects. Here is a closer look at this process.

The Lotus: Body Posture Makes a Difference

The recommended posture for meditation is called the 'lotus' posture, not because we look like a flower when we sit in this position, but because of the characteristics of the lotus blossom. Lotuses grow in muddy, stagnant water yet produce one of the most beautiful flowers in the world...even while meditating in the midst of the trials and tribulations and stagnant water of the material world, we can rise above it by entering the stillness within to a land of unsurpassable beauty.

To accomplish the lotus posture, sit as if you are going to cross your legs, and then place your right foot on your left thigh and your left foot on your right thigh. Straighten your back. Fold your hands in your lap with your fingers interlinked. Close your eyes and curl your tongue backwards against the roof of the mouth. This posture is ideal for meditation, as it keeps your back straight while promoting concentration and calmness of mind.

Of course many beginners in meditation find the lotus impossible, and adopt the half lotus posture (where the right leg is rested on the left), or they can sit in the even simpler cross-legged position.

The alternative postures provide almost the same benefits. If the cross-legged posture is still uncomfortable, sit on a cushion large enough to allow reasonable comfort with a straight back. If this is still not possible, meditate in a chair. For a beginning meditator, being reasonably comfortable and relaxed is more important than sitting correctly. Certainly avoid forcing your body into an uncomfortable position.

even while meditating in the midst of the trials and tribulations and stagnant water of the material world, we can rise above it by entering the stillness within to a land of unsurpassable beauty.

Sitting in lotus turns the mind inward. When we sit in lotus, or one of the other meditation postures, our sensory and motor organs automatically become less active. We close our eyes and shut off the visual. We choose a quiet place so we won't be distracted by sounds. Folding our hands and crossing our legs eliminates extraneous touch—just like a turtle withdrawn inside its shell. The tongue curled and pressed against the roof of the mouth deactivates the taste buds. If we have chosen our place well, smells will not bother us. Simply sitting still in such a posture without moving is in itself a powerful sensory withdrawal. By disengaging the mind from the senses, we are disconnecting it from the external world and giving ourselves an opportunity to dive deep inside. Motionlessness of the body leads to tranquillity of mind. When we close the doors of the senses, we get the chance to explore what is behind those doors.

Sitting motionless with our spine straight in the meditation posture is a simple technique, but it is not as easy as it might sound. In fact, most people find it quite difficult at first. Neither our bodies nor our minds are used to it—and they both may object vehemently. Yet, with perseverance we can become adept at sitting quietly in the meditation posture for extended periods of time. Once that is accomplished, we experience the power of these simple techniques to calm our minds and advance our inward journey.

Think of a rocket taking off. Most of the fuel is exhausted in the first few minutes with the explosive effort of overcoming the earth's gravitational forces. But once that inertia has been overcome as the rocket propels itself beyond its connection to the earth into orbital altitude, it travels great distances at high speeds with very little energy expenditure. Meditation's achievement of escape velocity to break out of the gravitational field of our day-to-day conscious mind requires great physical and mental energy, applied diligently. Keeping our spine straight and body quiet may be challenging, but it fuels the mind of the energy needed for take-off. A straight back increases the flow of blood to the brain (very important during meditation), while encouraging full deep breaths to increase the oxygenation of the blood. A straight back stimulates the subtle vital force in the body, which travels up the spine during meditation, known as chi or ki in China and Japan (as in Tai Chi or Ai-ki-do), and prana in India. Learning to concentrate or focus the mind and prevent it from running around wherever it wants is discussed in the next chapter and requires even more energy! Without this expenditure of energy, chances are we will never leave the ground.

> A straight back stimulates the subtle vital force in the body, which travels up the spine during meditation, known as chi or ki in China and Japan (as in Tai Chi or Ai-ki-do), and prana in India.

"Not once in a thousand times is it possible to achieve anything worth achieving except by labor, by effort, by serious purpose and by the willingness to take risks."
Theodore Roosevelt

Of course, there will still be some interaction between your mind and the external world while sitting in the lotus posture. After sitting quietly for a few minutes we may find that sounds and smells which we wouldn't ordinarily even notice start clamouring for our attention. If we find this happening, consider it the meditators version of withdrawal symptoms!

Are you Experiencing Withdrawal Symptoms?

We are accustomed to receiving a constant flow of information through our sensory organs. This stream of stimuli keeps us company from the moment we wake up until our last waking thought. Then we add our own distracting flavors to the mix through continuous and often subconscious inner dialogue. When we sit down for meditation and try to turn all the noise off, it is unfamiliar and contrary to our normal mental processes. We attempt to suddenly change the habits of an entire lifetime. Faced with the foreign experience of sensory deprivation, the mind instinctively grabs any stimulus available, just as a person caught in quicksand desperately to gropes for anything solid. We may suddenly become hypersensitive to every bit of sensory information that passes along our neuron pathways, which are still open of course.... Some of this information ordinarily would ordinarily never catch our attention. "Is that a phone ringing?" we ask ourselves of a faint sound in the distance. "What could that smell be?" Suddenly we detect an unrecognizable whiff of something in the air. No sooner do we embark on our inner journey than our conscious mind, unaccustomed to quietness, strives to return to what it knows best: paying attention to and focusing on what is going on 'out there.'

"I bet it was Sue. Maybe there's been an accident. I should have picked up . . ."

"I think I hear Jack bringing in the mail...maybe that application has finally arrived...with all the things I have to do, I can't sit here and meditate...I'll try another time."

Normally, thoughts run through our mind like a herd of wild horses. As long as they are untamed, they continue to do whatever they want, and what they enjoy most is going for rides with the help of our senses— meeting people, watching what's going on, enjoying the sights and sounds of a fascinating world. If we fence our thoughts in through a process of sensory withdrawal, they rush to find an open exit. If they don't find an open door, panic sets in and they'll jump the fence or squeeze through any small opening. This initial effect on the mind of the sensory withdrawal process underscores our craving for sensory input; at the same time it dawns on us how little control we actually exert over our thoughts.

This mental response when it first starts withdrawing from the senses is characteristic of any addict deprived of their addictive substance, whether it be food, drugs, applause—whatever. Our minds, dependent on this sensory stimulation, crave it as deeply as an addict. 'Hooked' on the world outside us, we find it so difficult for us to sit quietly for 20 or 30 minutes to explore our inner world.

Fed up with Sensory Stimulation

We can be so addicted to external stimulation that we experience sensory overload— burnout. Think of all those around you who can't— or won't—go more than an hour without putting something in their mouth—a cigarette, coffee or chocolate. These oftentimes unconscious, compulsive actions deeply engage the sensory and motor organs. Being almost the only creatures to eat when not hungry, humans literally get 'fed up.'

Obsessive behaviours in other areas of our lives similarly affect us. When we fail to develop our inner resources, we constantly 'feed ourselves' with stimuli as a means to keep ourselves happy—or at least stave off depression. But this dependency leads to a vicious cycle that may be difficult to break. We need more and more stimulation to get the same effect—five cups of coffee becomes eight and the single daily smoke develops into two packs of cigarettes. The more we take in, the stronger our dependency and the less able we are to break away. This vicious circle eventually fosters fatigue, anxiety, nervous disorders and mental breakdown.

> *"We have tested and tasted too much love*
> *Through a chink too wide there comes in no wonder*
> *But here...*
> *We will charm back the luxury of a child's soul."*
>   W. H. Auden

Do you remember how good things tasted as a child? How full of mystery and wonder the world was! By the time we reach adulthood we become so accustomed to the sensory universe that we dismiss the freshness, the mystery, and the beauty of the world around us.

The practice of sensory withdrawal gradually changes that decline. It weans us from dependence on objects of self-gratification, helps us gain control of our senses, root out our obsessions and restore the sense of wonder we enjoyed as children. By recapturing the magic of a child's innocence, even the simple things in life fill us with joy. Rather than denying the external world, meditation rejuvenates and restores our appreciation of our senses, just as fasting for even a few hours gives us a healthy appetite and imparts sweeter flavors to our foods. After meditation, we experience the beauty of the wonderful sights and sounds of this world with renewed interest, as though we had just come back from a holiday. And indeed we have.

Sensory withdrawal is just the beginning. It's the push that takes our boat out of the harbor. If wind in the sail is sensory withdrawal, the rudder that controls and unlocks our minds is concentration.

> By recapturing the magic of a child's innocence, even the simple things in life fill us with joy.

68

Try This

•Find a peaceful place somewhere outside in nature where you will not be disturbed. Sit there for a few minutes, without closing your eyes, just tuning in to the feeling of harmony around you. Now close your eyes and notice how your body and your breathing are also a part of nature's harmony. The blood flows and nerves work all by themselves, you breath automatically, it all happens by itself almost miraculously. Now just watch your breathing, and focus on this sense of inner harmony. Sit like this for ten minutes or more.

•Write down your observations in your meditation journal.

"...And I have felt
A presence that disturbs me with the joy
Of elevated thoughts; a sense sublime
Of something far more deeply interfused,
Whose dwelling is the light of setting suns,
And the round ocean and the living air
And the blue sky, and in the mind of man;
A motion and a spirit, that impels
All thinking things, all objects of all thought,
and rolls through all things...."

William Wordsworth

Chapter Four

Developing Concentration

"While doing meditation, the mind frequently runs after external things; it is extremely difficult to focus exclusively on only one object or idea. Why do we concentrate on a particular point during meditation? Because that point is the link between the relative world and the Absolute; the point exists where the relative world ends and the Absolute begins. It represents the Cosmic Entity. Once this point is controlled, the attainment of the highest state of spirituality becomes easy. Therefore, in order to withdraw the mind from the relative world, we must concentrate on this point."

Shrii Shrii Anandamurti

Now that we have withdrawn our mind from our senses by sitting quietly in lotus (or cross-legged) posture, we're about to set sail on our voyage into the deep interior. Sensory withdrawal raises the anchor holding us to our mundane lives, and casts us off.

But before we even leave the harbor we discover a host of unruly thoughts on board— stowaways who are not the least bit interested in the voyage. They instead crave fame, fortune and a ripping good time (and prospects for that don't look good on this ship). Like a band of rogue pirates, they sabotage. They fight against their would-be captain (you) and themselves, each pulling in a different direction. Heading into the sunset with this band of ruffians, you wonder what you have let yourself in for.

"A country can be conquered by force of arms, but the mind cannot."

Shrii Shrii Anandamurti

Take a closer look at this unruly mob of thoughts that plague our conscious minds. To deal with them effectively, we must first understand their nature.

According to Yogic science, the mind has three predominant characteristics:

1. The mind must have an object.
2. The mind can only think of one thing at a time.
3. As you think so you become.

1. The Mind Must have an Object.

It would be wonderful if we could just sit down in meditation and stop thinking altogether, without a single ripple in the mind to prevent us from experiencing total peace and tranquillity. Unfortunately it is not so easy.

Try it for a moment. Close your eyes and try to make your mind blank.

Any luck? Even if you managed to avoid getting caught up in your problems, preoccupations or aimless thoughts for a few precious seconds, you would likely still have had some image in your mind—the room, your surroundings, the colors behind your eyelids. You had an awareness of yourself in those surroundings. You felt some emotion. Perhaps you were aware of your breathing. Almost certainly something was in your mind. If there wasn't, then there is no need for you to read the rest of this book or learn how to meditate, because you have already achieved what meditators spend a lifetime striving to achieve: inner peace, or the ability to make the mind completely still at will.

When the mind merges completely with pure consciousness, the meditator enters a state of bliss. Some adepts attain the capacity to enter this Yogic trance at will, but it is rare and, universally, they achieve this after years of effort. More on bliss in later chapters...

Until one attains these higher states of mind, ripples continue in the mind because the mind must have an object. It requires something to think about if it is to exist in the first place. As long as your awareness of your Self or 'I' continues to exist, the 'not-I' or what is outside your sense of self, also continues to exist. This is the nature of the mind; there is no escape.

While (for the time being) you have no choice about whether you think, you do have enormous choice about what you think. What we think affects our mind in an array of ways.

The Inner Tape Recorder

> "You say so many things, and major portions of what you say
> are meaningless, simply a waste of time and energy. And not
> only that, but you also talk inside your mind. And that is a
> waste of energy too. Before going to Stockholm, you may say
> a thousand times in your mind, 'I have to go to Stockholm;
> I have to go to Stockholm; I am to go to Stockholm' a sheer
> waste of time and energy. What is thought? Thought means

to talk in your mind. Thought is closely related to soliloquy. Suppose there is nobody to hear you and you are talking. What is it? It is just like a thought. When you are talking to yourself, it is called 'soliloquy.' Thought is also like that. Some of your thoughts are such that, if others hear them, they will say you are insane."

Shrii Shrii Anandamurti

We talk to ourselves all day long. Some of it is conscious, but much is sub-conscious, hidden just below the surface of ordinary awareness. We conduct conversations with people we may or may not know; we have discussions with ourselves. This internal dialogue emphasizes our fears and complexes and sabotages our peace of mind. We sit down to take a test and tell ourselves that we can't possibly pass. We may not even notice that sub-conscious voice inside us, but it does its damage all the same. This internal tape recorder goes 24 hours a day. We can't turn it off. We can't even turn the volume down. We don't always pay attention to it, but there it is, in the background affecting how we feel, what we say, what we do. At times it gets so annoying that it's as if we've tuned into a radio station we don't like but can't switch off.

The first thing we easily understand about the mind: it really likes to think.

2. The Mind Can Only Think About One Thing at a Time.

Yes the mind loves to think, yet it cannot think of more than one thing at a time.

Try as you like, two thoughts cannot occupy the same mental space at the same instant. You cannot hold two images or repeat two words simultaneously: what actually happens is the mind jumps about at incredible speed. The effect is somewhat like that of a motion picture, composed of a series of still images changing so rapidly (24 to 30 frames per second) that the objects appear to move. All perception—visual, auditory, tactile, taste, smell—functions as a series of discrete 'snapshots' that seem continuous only because the gap between them is

The second characteristic of the mind: it thinks of just one thing at a time. Often considered a limitation of the mind, it is also its great strength. This characteristic enables concentration.

minute, too small for our sensory receptors to register as separate.

The second characteristic of the mind: it thinks of just one thing at a time. Often considered a limitation of the mind, it is also its great strength. This characteristic enables concentration.

Living in the Future

Mental energy is intimately bound up with desires and aspirations; many of our thoughts are concerned with an imaginary future. 'If I can only pull off this job...I wonder what she'll be wearing...I hope it doesn't rain tomorrow, that would really spoil things...if I could just find a good teacher then I know I could make it...' When our imagination is urged on by anxieties or fears, we dread the worst rather than visualize the best. Our imagination counters every good reason for success with more bad reasons for failure and then previews them in an internal cinema. 'If this doesn't work out, then that's bound to go wrong...Yikes...I don't even want to think about what might happen.' But of course we do—think and then think some more.

Although we like to believe that our predictions are accurate, they more often are fantasy fiction—and we spend hours of mental effort in writing and rewriting that fiction into a work that never gets published. Compared to the fantastic creations of our imagination, actual events are rendered as boring. Our imagination makes golf-ball sized difficulties into an avalanche of tragedy. Yet in reality, most of what we fear, predict or assume never happens; the future has the habit of summarily destroying the best laid plans

> *"My life has been full of the most terrible tragedies, most of which never occurred."*
> Dale Carnegie

Complicated People

One consequence of this living-in-the-future mentality is people live as if the present had importance only as preparation for an imagined future. Young people want to get older while our elders wish for youth. Personalities fragment strangely. A politician may think one thing, say another, and do something completely different in order to win an election. It is the same with us. When we speak and act purely from the perspective of what benefit might result, we become complicated. We seldom say what we really feel for fear of the consequences, and we lie to others—and ourselves.

"Suppose your boss arrives. You welcome him saying, 'Please come in, sit down and have something to eat.' You flatter him externally, but inside you say, 'What a nuisance! When will he go?' Your boss does not know this. Thus, you have two 'I's inside you: one performs actions in the external world, while the other thinks something different inside. You are well acquainted with this inner 'I,' but others do not have a correct perception of it. This is what we call the two faces of a single personality, a psychic disease. The greater the gap between these two 'I's, the more psychic torment a person will suffer. You must remember that in this second half of the 20th Century there is a great gap between the internal 'I' and the external 'I.' And because of the trouble in adjusting these two 'I's there is an increase in the number of lunatics. This is the greatest disease of the 20th Century."

Shrii Shrii Anandamurti

Living in the Past

When our minds are not engaged in thinking about the future, we usually dwell on the past. This tendency increases with age. While some of our memories are pleasant often it is the painful events that haunt us the most. 'She had no right to speak to me like that...It's his fault that everything is going wrong...I wish I had never done that... now look at the mess I'm in...' If we feel we have been wronged we usually find ourselves explaining our side of the story to someone else. But of course there is no one there: it is only the ravings of our inner soliloquy, rehearsing our lines before an empty stage. We might waste our time replaying events and emotions in our heads repeatedly like a television junkie watching re-runs of I Love Lucy. Painful memories might develop into a dominant part of our self-image, effectively barring us from healthy, joyous experiences in daily life, even though they have no more substance than a mirage in a burning desert.

Living in the Present

One morning I sat at the breakfast table watching a friend of mine gulping down his toast and coffee, reading the newspaper and putting on his coat—all at the same time. Every few seconds he anxiously glanced up at the clock and mumbled something about how late he was for work. When I asked him how breakfast was he had nothing to say except that he was 'on his way out.' "Was there anything interesting in the paper today?" I asked. "Don't know," he replied. "Take it. I'm out of here."

Yet 'here' was where his life was taking place. What a waste that he should choose to be marked absent at that precious moment. There was no tasting the food he was eating or absorbing the headlines he was reading because he was mentally 'on the way out.' His body was going through the motions; his mind was elsewhere. He might as well have eaten the newspaper. Later that day I watched the Spanish Formula One Grand Prix on TV—the most exciting race I ever saw. After an initial surge that put Michael Schumacher way ahead of the field, he suddenly slowed down as one car after another passed him. His pit crew told the commentators that he was stuck in

> It is only here, in this precious, fleeting moment that we are truly and fully alive. That fraction of an instant—the eternal 'now' living in the gap between past and future—comes and goes so swiftly that most of us miss it.

fifth gear. Yet, rather than give up and pull out, Schumacher declared to the pits that he would to finish the race to gain points for the world championship. Incredibly enough, in ten laps he started to overtake the other cars and moved into second place.

The television commentators could not believe that he was driving with only one gear. If he were, then how could he possibly be picking up speed out of the turns? They stopped the running commentary to let us all listen for any change of gear via the live video camera on Schumacher's car. For the next half lap millions of people throughout the world saw and heard just what Schumacher was experiencing as he hurtled down the straightway into the turn at breathtaking speed.

There was no change of gear! I sat on the edge of my seat looking through Schumacher's windshield as it flew into the turn at 150 miles per hour. With no gear change slow him down, his car wavered almost uncontrollably. I could feel the excitement and exhilaration, almost as if I were sitting in the car with him, and the tremendous courage it took to be doing what he was doing.

Whatever Schumacher was thinking of as he hurtled down the straightway at 200 miles an hour, it was not dinner, the next race or his next public appearance. Riding into the wind on a fragile piece of metal, he was focused on that moment as if his life depended on it—as it did.

"I must have waited all my life for this
Moment... moment... moment..."
                                    Jon Anderson

It is only here, in this precious, fleeting moment that we are truly and fully alive. That fraction of an instant—the eternal 'now' living in the gap between past and future—comes and goes so swiftly that most of us miss it. Yet if we are fully awake at that instant, we find ourselves immersed in an experience so rich that no creation of our imagination can possibly equal it. Only when we fully awaken in the present do we experience the vastness of life's offerings.

If, during his dramatic run to the finish line, Schumacher had not been fully present, mentally and emotionally he would not have survived. Our situation is not as different as we might think. If we cannot be truly present as our life unfolds, we will not survive but join the ranks of the living dead. We miss out on why we came here. Truly speaking, we are alive only to the extent that we are mentally present in each and every moment.

"Life is what happens to you while you're busy making other
plans."
                                    John Lennon

The practice of concentration and meditation disciplines our mind, to keep it from brooding over the sins of the past or wasting our precious energy on the phantasms of an imaginary future. Slowly, slowly, we begin to feel a tremendous sense of power. We feel more awake, alive and uplifted. We become conscious participants in our life, awake to the infinite possibilities inherent in each moment. Whatever we choose to do, we do wholeheartedly with full attention. No matter how mundane the task, even if we are only doing the laundry, it becomes filled with the joy and vitality of conscious living. The better our concentration becomes, the smaller the gap between what we do and what we think... until it disappears. We then feel the Oneness of all things.

"Oh body swayed to music,
O brightening glance
How can we know the dancer from the dance?"
                                    W. B. Yeats

The secret of true concentration: living in the present. When we focus the energy of our minds through concentration, we discover the power of the mind.

3. As You Think so You Become.

"Your imagination is your preview of life's coming attractions."
Albert Einstein

"Imagination is the beginning of creation. You imagine what you desire; you will what you imagine, and at last you create what you will."

George Bernard Shaw

The power of our thoughts in shaping our reality has been recognized by great thinkers in all cultures throughout history. Thoughts not only shape our reality, they are our reality—the mind is where we experience the external world. All the brilliant inventions of mankind, both for good and for evil, began as seeds in the imagination and took birth when the mind turned those seeds into physical reality. The mind is the creative force behind all our achievements. Thoughts are not simply idle mental gossip—they are powerful creative potentialities, seeking expression in the external world. Look deeply into our world of events and objects to find someone's thought at the root of everything, from the red light that orders you to stop your car to the stroke of bad luck which you swear was an accident.

> If our thoughts are strong or persistent enough, they become the landscape through which our road passes, which is not always the terrain that we desired.

Our attitudes color our experience; they dictate what we see and don't see. Recall the old adage that if a saint walks down the street, a pickpocket sees only his pockets. Thoughts guide us down the road of life as we struggle to materialize our hopes and desires. If our thoughts are strong or persistent enough, they become the landscape through which our road passes, which is not always the terrain that we desired. Most importantly, our thoughts are responsible for who we are, for our weaknesses and strengths, our foibles and talents, our capacity to love, to endure suffering and to derive joy, from each moment in the drama of our existence. Buddha said:

"We are what we think, having become what we have thought."

The increasing emphasis on positive thinking prevalent in current Western society has roots in this third characteristic of the mind. If we indulge in negative thoughts, we develop negative mental tendencies, and this not only creates anxiety, tension and fear, but it sabotages our efforts to get ahead. By consciously striving toward positive thoughts, we increase our sense of well-being while creating a congenial environment for the actual materialization of those thoughts in our daily lives. Mary Baker Eddy successfully demonstrated the power of positive affirmations in the healing of disease.

In order to utilise this characteristic of the mind to our advantage, we must exercise some control over what we think. We must train the mind to avoid getting lost and taking us astray. An untrained mind is like a frisky young dog that dashes around madly the moment you let go of the leash. If we let the mind wander according to its natural tendency, it will pull us in many different directions, leaving us dizzy and confused, at the mercy of whimsical thoughts and conflicting desires. Thoughts generally concern themselves with an imaginary future and a dead yet unburied past. If we are to train the mind properly, one of the first things we need to learn is to live in the present.

Concentration

Do you remember that student in your fifth grade class who couldn't concentrate? Every classroom has one. While the teacher discusses the fall of the Roman Empire, he is sending off a note, fidgeting with his pencil or turning around at the slightest sound. No matter how often the teacher asks him to pay attention, it never lasts. A minute later his mind is wandering again, or a sound or a movement from one of the other students distracts him. Do you remember this student? Well that student was you—and it still is. How often, while you speak with a friend, are you actually thinking about the concert you have tickets for that evening, the one you've been looking forward to all week? Or, sitting in the office listening to a colleague's

> The basis of all meditation-indeed of all conscious life-is the art of concentration, the capacity to focus our attention on one thing.

presentation, your mind wanders off to a conversation you had at lunch? Or you're midway through the second song of the concert, and you imagine yourself onstage with the guitar in your hands and the audience going wild—instead of really listening to the music? The mind simply can't stay put, no matter how much or how politely we ask it. Some people do have it. A childhood friend of mine had an amazing capacity to become absorbed in a book to the exclusion of all else. His sisters and I made a game of it: we gesticulated about him loudly, insulting him, laughing and trying to make him notice us, but he was totally oblivious. He was so focused that he couldn't hear us.

What is concentration? It is as simple as giving your full attention to one thing and keeping it there, be it an absorbing book, a friendly conversation, an inspiring piece of music or the beauty of the sun setting over the ocean. It is simple, but by no means easy. If you can concentrate, you have mastered the secret of living in the present, for when you are able to give your whole attention to what you are doing, you become fully awake in the moment. Your inner 'I' and your outer 'I' become one; your mind acquires tremendous power. Its ordinary, scattered state it is just like the diffuse rays of the sun: warm but not particularly powerful. Concentrate those rays through a large enough magnifying glass and they will burn a hole through stone.

Paramahansa Yogananda, the great Indian Yogi, was accosted in Los Angeles by an armed robber who ordered him to hand over his money. "Put that gun down immediately," Yogananda said, and his words had such force that the robber threw down his weapon and fled. Someone with a concentrated mind is able to command more than just respect.

The basis of all meditation—indeed of all conscious life—is the art of concentration, the capacity to focus our attention on one thing. When the object of concentration is our awareness, the infinite Self within all of us, that is meditation. The deeper our concentration, the more we are penetrate to the secret of who we are.

Concentration in Meditation

Meditation takes advantage of the fact that we can only think of one thing at a time. This actually makes our task simpler. As long as the mind is engaged in one thought it cannot think about anything else; if it is engaged in the present it cannot get lost in the past or the future. All we have to do is repeat the same thought over and over again, like an hourglass with single grains of sand falling through, one after another, in a steady unbroken flow.

The way meditation accomplishes this is to choose a single idea of concentration. When the mind wanders away from this idea, we bring it back. It wanders away again, and

> Meditation takes advantage of the fact that we can only think of one thing at a time. This actually makes our task simpler.

again we bring it back. We don't force it to remain focused by pushing other thoughts away, nor do we let it wander freely. We simply bring it back to our one idea once we become aware that it has wandered away, time after time, session after session, day after day. Over time our mind develops the habit of returning to this idea.

In the beginning our mind may only stay focused for very short periods of time, a few seconds perhaps and it may drift for some time before we even notice that it has wandered. But each time we bring it back we strengthen the habit. Gradually, due to the forced repetition, the mind becomes accustomed to this practice. The gap is reduced; we catch the mind much sooner when it does wander. Eventually we develop the ability to focus for long periods of time. Distractions still come and go but they lose their hold over us. They lose their ability to divert our minds from our point of concentration. The mind's ability to maintain and deepen its concentration develops tremendous force.

Practice this concentration technique with virtually any object as a focus. It can be something external like a candle flame, a spot on the wall, or something internal like a particular image or a particular sound. However, as we learned when we looked at the third characteristic of the mind, 'as we think so we become,' our choice of concentration topic is vitally important. We are free to choose any object of concentration, but our choice drives who we become in the process. For concentration to become meditation, our focus of concentration must be our Inner Self, the goal of our long voyage through life. More on this in the next chapter...

Unlocking the Door to Self-Discovery

> In the depths of our own minds hides the secret of who we are: our innermost, and as yet undiscovered, Self.

Once a teenage girl told me that she was very concerned about what other people thought about her. I reassured her, "don't worry, it really isn't a problem. Generally, other people are not thinking about you at all. They are too busy worrying what you think about them." We are all like that. What is the first thing you do when you look at an old class photo? Who is the most interesting person in the world to you?

One natural aid to the art of concentration is to choose something interesting to concentrate on. When the movie is boring or the conversation turns to a mundane topic, it becomes more difficult to keep your attention fixed on it. When we meditate let's choose what is, for all of us, the most interesting thing in the universe. (If you are shown your high school class graduation photo, who will you look for first? We all know the answer to that question.) Our own self is—always will be—the real object of our search. Self-discovery is what meditation is all about because that is what the journey of life is all about.

At first meditation is the ocean when it has been stirred up by a storm. The water is murky and laden with silt and mud, and we cannot see into its depths. We cannot even see how deep it might be. But if we are patient, the mud slowly clears, and the vast undersea world with all its wonders reveals itself. In the depths of our own minds hides the secret of who we are: our innermost, and as yet undiscovered, Self.

When I was relatively new to the art of meditation, I learned something about how concentration helps one's meditation practice. I was on my way to teach an introductory meditation class, and I had about two hours to spare. As I was near a beautiful beach in Noosa, Australia as sunset approached, I decided to meditate on the beach. It was an idyllic spot. Small waves were breaking gently on the sand, and dolphins were playing in the water. It seemed like a perfect setting.

But no sooner had I closed my eyes than I felt a tickling sensation on my hands and then on my arms and face, and an unpleasant stinging sensation on several spots of my exposed skin. Mosquitoes! I opened my eyes and to my dismay saw a dozen mosquitoes feeding on me with a cloud of fifty more hovering nearby. How ironic that this perfect spot should be infested with these bloodsuckers. I brushed them away but they were not at all discouraged and invited their friends. This was hopeless! I was not getting any meditation done at all.

I took a firm determination to close my eyes and meditate for one hour without moving even if the mosquitoes sucked me completely dry. At first it was incredibly difficult. I visualized their terrible little noses poking into my flesh and drinking my blood. Desperate to react, I steeled my will and started my meditation. After just a few minutes I became deeply absorbed in one of the most blissful meditation experiences ever and thought no more of the mosquitoes for the next hour. When I opened my eyes, the mosquitoes were gone. I was amazed to find not one bite.

> When this happens, we experience a profound sense of inner joy, wisdom, peace and clarity, far deeper than anything we have ever known.

I realized then: I could concentrate anytime if I really wanted to.

With the Inner Self as our object of concentration, we turn our mind inwards. As our experience of meditation becomes more blissful, our mind is naturally attracted to this mysterious Inner Self. Gradually, through regular practice, the stream of our consciousness gets focused in this direction. All our emotions and thoughts flow together towards the vast inner regions of the mind. When this happens, we experience a profound sense of inner joy, wisdom, peace and clarity, far deeper than anything we have ever known. From the conscious mind to the subconscious mind and deeper still, concentration in meditation is the key which unlocks the door to that wondrous inner Self.

Try This

•Return to your meditation spot out in nature (if the weather is too bad you can find a place indoors). This time, with your eyes open, choose something to focus on. A tree or a leaf or a stone – it does not matter what. Keep your gaze fixed on this and become aware of your breathing. Do this for ten minutes. Then do the closed eyes meditation, focusing on your breathing and trying to keep your mind in the present moment, only in the present.

•Observe how your mind tends to wander away from the present moment. See if you can catch yourself thinking of something seemingly random, and then trace the 'thought chain', that led you to that thought. Note in your journal how your mind keeps creating these chains where one thought leads to another and to another. Begin to develop some self-awareness around this mental habit, and how it keeps us from remaining focused in the present.

"You opened new doorways,
Shining on the world
I beheld You in the heart of dreams
This time the magic will never die."

From the song The Return of the Magic,
by the author

Chapter Five

Mantra: The Song of the Inner World

"Without depending upon Mantra... Buddhahood cannot be attained."

Dalai Lama

Thinking of our own consciousness

Imagine the countryside at night. It has been raining, but the clouds have cleared, revealing the moon. A few cows saunter by in the pale light. They leave footprints in the soft earth, and as water fills the indentations, they form a series of tiny pools with the moon reflected in each one. There appear to be many moons, yet anyone who looks up at the sky understands that they are all simply reflections of the one moon. The feeling that 'I know that I exist,' our individual consciousness, is known as the Atman in Samskrta. Materialists argue that consciousness is a product of chemical processes, but no scientist on Earth has been able to explain this. Yogis long ago realized that the entire universe is a thought projection of Cosmic Consciousness; what we call 'reality,' from the perspective of the creator, is thought. Our individual minds reflect this Cosmic Consciousness, making us aware of our own existence. Like the moons reflected in the water, my 'I' feeling, and your 'I' feeling are reflections of the same Cosmic 'I.' The experience of this pure 'I' feeling, independent of any thought, is the goal of our meditation.

> Our individual minds reflect this Cosmic Consciousness, making us aware of our own existence.

But how can we concentrate on pure consciousness, on something that is infinite? The only thing that the eye cannot see is the eye itself; in the case of the mind, it is the 'I' that cannot see the 'I.' How can the mind reach that which is beyond the mind, out of which the mind arises? This is the meditator's dilemma.

"A blade cuts things
But not itself:
Eyes see everything
But themselves."

A Zen Forest. Sayings of the Masters,
Translated by Soiku Shigematsu

Thousands of years ago yogis in India discovered the solution to this dilemma. They found a method that could bring the restless mind to a state of transcendental peace. The method was Mantra.

The word Mantra comes from ancient Sanskrit, literally meaning 'that which liberates the mind.' Man means 'mind' and tra means 'freedom,' so a Mantra is a word or a group of several words which, when meditated upon, leads the mind to freedom. It transports us through the maze of our thoughts to the ocean of pure consciousness. How does it do this?

When we meditate, we must think about something; that is, an object of concentration. In this case, it is a word, a meaningful sound vibration with the capacity to create a certain type of rhythm in our mind. All Mantras used for meditation possess these three characteristics: sound, rhythm and meaning. Each signifies specific roles in the context of Mantra meditation.

1. The Power of Sound

As I write these words I am listening to a recording of a spiritual chant—Flow of Love by Sukha Deva, one of the finest musicians I know of. How can such a simple thing have such a powerful, mysteriously potent effect? With no effort on my part, the music awakens a blissful feeling in my heart, soft but joyful. It is so strange—as a Yogi and a musician, I understand the theory of why this is happening, yet the power of these sounds to transform my mood in a moment still seems magical.

Sound is the origin of all things.

The mythologies of many cultures tell of sound at the Dawn of Time—that the Creator used music to weave the cosmic spell. The Old Testament of the Bible relates, "In the beginning was the Word." Australian Aboriginal tradition tells how the Universe was 'sung' into being, and the Tibetan Book of the Dead reveals the essence of reality as "reverberating like a thousand distant thunders."

In yoga philosophy the first vibration—the primordial sound of the Universe—is the Aum (or Om) sound. This sound represents the sum total of all of the vibrations in the universe, embodying

In deep meditation it is possible to hear this sound, the Om sound, the seed sound of the entire Universe reverberating in our innermost being.

within it the three aspects of God as Brahma the Creator, Vishnu the Preserver and Maheshvara the Destroyer. In deep meditation it is possible to hear this sound, the Om sound, the seed sound of the entire Universe reverberating in our innermost being. According to physics the universe began with a vast explosion of energy—a Big Bang. There are many parallels between creation myths and the emerging discoveries of modern physicists.

Vibration has great power—remember the biblical story of the walls of Jericho being brought down by the blowing of trumpets? When soldiers cross a bridge they fall out of step to prevent the regular rhythm of their marching from setting up a resonance that causes the bridge to sway higher and higher until it shakes itself to pieces.

music is used in most spiritual or religious traditions to induce devotional trances, ecstasy and altered states of consciousness.

Sound and music heal. In the 5th Century BC, Democritus of Greece wrote of snake bites cured by the playing of a flute. American and European therapy centers use music to help Alzheimer's, Parkinson's and cancer patients. Music producer Terry Woodford uses recordings of the human heartbeat blended into the rhythm of the music, to help children and adult patients in more than 4,000 hospitals.

We see the same principle at work in the magical rituals and practices of indigenous people, in tribal chanting and in magical spells. India holds an ancient tradition of healing through music, with incredible tales of a violinist curing terminally ill patients through music.

The great Indian musician, Tansen, in order to please his king, caused a tree to burst into blossom out of season by playing a particular Raga on his veena (a multi-stringed classical instrument, a little like a sitar).

Most significantly, considering our subject, music is used in most spiritual or religious traditions to induce devotional trances, ecstasy and altered states of consciousness.

Sound Affects Our Emotions

We are most sensitive to sound. The ear is the first sensory organ to develop and it is fully functional halfway through gestation, four and a half months before birth. Sounds heard in the womb stimulate development of the nervous system. We all experience the capacity of sound to effect changes in our mental state. The sound of the sea is sometimes melancholic; the sound of a flowing river makes us feel serene, while the sound of a chainsaw sets our nerves on edge. A Bach prelude, a baby crying or someone scraping their nails on a blackboard all affect our mind in distinctly different ways. Different sounds can induce completely different emotions in us, almost instantaneously. The same is true for form and color. Sit quietly for some time in a light blue room then move to a bright red room and you will notice a marked change in your mental state. This is why mental health centers are usually painted light blue, or light green. It is hard to imagine anyone painting them red or black!

Everything that we perceive has an effect on the mind, and it is this fundamental universal law that makes the use of Mantra so effective.

Mantra and Chakras

If you go out in the countryside at night in clear weather, you may be dazzled by the brilliant light of thousands of stars scattered like jewels upon the ocean of the night. Yet the next morning they are gone. The sky is blue. We know the stars are there but the sun, so much nearer, outshines them.

Not everything that is real is visible. We never see some things that are real, like the wind, or the electromagnetic field surrounding the earth...or people's thoughts.

If we go down to the deep, quiet part of the mind, we begin to experience its hidden wonders. As the ancient Yogis observed how different sounds affect our thoughts and feelings, they developed a subtle intuitive understanding of the relationship between sounds and our body, vital energy and mental state. Studying the body and mind, they gained insights into health, psychology and spiritual practice. This is their basis for the science of Mantra.

According to the Yogic model, our physical body is just one aspect of the multi-dimensional human system. Parallel to the physical body is a more subtle body of vital energy or prana ('chi' in Chinese philosophy). The flow of this vital energy throughout our system regulates our health, vitality, thinking and emotions. This is not a physical force—you cannot find it if you cut open the body—yet it flows in definite patterns in the body and that are

> In high states of meditation this subtle energy body can actually be perceived as a pattern of brilliant channels of energy and glittering colored lotuses along the spinal column at the points where the energy channels intersect.

Diagram of chakras, nadis and vrtis of the human system.
Illustration by Jagadiish Azzopardi

felt when we develop the right sensitivity. There are three main channels of vital energy. One runs through the center of the spinal column. The other two originate one behind each nostril and in their downward flow they weave back and forth across the spine. The points where they intersect are the Chakras. Seven major Chakras reside in the vicinity of major glands that influence our emotions through hormonal secretions. It is this Chakra system that forms the connection between our physical bodies, nervous system, glands and our minds. For example, the third Chakra near the adrenal glands at the navel point is related (among other things) to hunger and fear.

In high states of meditation this subtle energy body can actually be perceived as a pattern of brilliant channels of energy and glittering colored lotuses along the spinal column at the points where the energy channels intersect. Each lotus petal corresponds to a particular human propensity, desire or feeling, and each emits a corresponding color and sound.

> "The best and most beautiful things in the world cannot be
> seen or even touched. They must be felt within the heart."
> Helen Keller

Vrtiis—Mental Propensities

Our mental activity is an enormously complex matrix of desires and feelings, but the process through which thoughts arise is not random. At the core of our psyche are fifty principle propensities (vrttis in Sanskrit). Each emotion or desire we feel—such as fear, anger, compassion, affection or shyness—is the expression of one of these propensities. Some are mundane physical desires based on survival instincts. Others are more subtle, reflecting our mental evolution, and still others are sublime expressions of our fundamental spiritual yearning. To regulate these propensities is to gain control of our minds.

Think for a moment of the process of color photography. Three colors—blue, red and yellow—are mixed together in various intensities; the combination of these three colors gives rise to the millions of colors of the visible spectrum when we look at a photograph, painting, or simply open our eyes to the world around us. The human mind has not three but fifty psychic colors or propensities, each of which can be expressed at many levels of intensity. One or more of these mental propensities is almost always active to some degree in every individual. The combinations of propensities active at any given time generate a variety of thoughts and feelings. When all the propensities become completely still, Pure Consciousness shines in its original, unaltered state and the meditator enters the blissful state of trance known as Samadhi.

Sanskrit – the language of Mantras

As the investigations of the ancient Yogis took them deeper into the subtle realms of the mind, they found sound and its meaning—the domain of language at the very root of human thought processes. Not only did they discover that language is the prime determinant of how we perceive the world, they also found that each of the fifty vrttis, controlled by the seven Chakras, had a corresponding sound.

These fifty sounds make up the fifty letters of the Sanskrit alphabet. It is because of this intimate link with the human psyche that Sanskrit is ideally suited for the creation of Mantras for meditation and spiritual practice.

A student related the wonderfully strange experience that when he sits for meditation, he did not need to repeat the Mantra because he hears it coming from deep within his own mind.

Yogis studying science of Mantra realized that this was a powerful tool in the quest for spiritual liberation. Some of our fifty mental propensities are deeply introversial. The sound of the Mantra awakens these—the purest, most uplifting of our innermost feelings. The Mantra guides us towards infinite consciousness.

> These fifty sounds make up the fifty letters of the Sanskrit alphabet. It is because of this intimate link with the human psyche that Sanskrit is ideally suited for the creation of Mantras for meditation and spiritual practice.

> "There's a song I'm told that has no music,
> And an ocean without waves,
> There's a peace that passeth all understanding,
> And I long to find it so."

From the song Shanti, by the author

2. Breathing

The next characteristic of a Mantra is that it is rhythmic. What this means on the practical level is that it aligns with our breathing, and therefore all Mantras for personal meditation consist of two syllables.

Our breathing exerts a great influence over our thinking. The more rapid and irregular our breathing, the more difficult it becomes for us to concentrate deeply. When our breathing slows down, our capacity to think deeply increases. Ask a question of someone who has just been running for some distance and is breathing very heavily. They will probably say, "Hang on a minute while I catch my breath." Conversely, whenever you are deeply concentrating on any subject, you will notice that your breathing is very slow and regular.

The alignment of the Mantra with our breathing has two principle benefits: firstly, it helps to naturally regulate and slow our breathing, which in turn deepens our concentration; and secondly, an association develops between our breathing and the repetition of the Mantra, which helps us to remember the Mantra. When people become accomplished in this practice, they find that the Mantra continues with their breath even when they are not formally meditating. Their minds remain in a meditative state even while they go about their daily activities. When they sit for meditation, they find it easy to remain concentrated, because the Mantra is already rising and falling with their breath.

3. The Meaning of the Mantra

"Without ideational concept, the repetition of a Mantra is a waste of time."

Shrii Shrii Anandamurti

The Power of Thinking – Your Mental Object.

Thinking, as we normally understand it, involves a subject and an object. Take this one step further, and distinguish between our mental object (or the image we have in our mind of something external to us) and the object itself (even if the mental object is an abstract concept). The thing our mental object refers to (that new car, your name in all the fashion magazines) may not exist yet in reality. It may never exist. But the thought exists, and thoughts are, after all, significant events involving movements of powerful energy. Space shuttles and nuclear weapons began as thoughts within the human mind—the most powerful device in the known universe.

A small group of semi-autistic children suffered from arrested development. They had not been able to make the essential transition from crawling to walking—although there was no physical reason for not walking, they were unable to take the mental first step despite the best efforts of their teachers. One of the teachers had an idea: he taught them a new game. He tied a rope between two heavy chairs, and got the children to stand, holding the rope for support. They could stand when supported. Then he taught them to start taking steps supported by the rope, and they played at this until they could traverse the entire length of the rope. Each day he substituted a thinner rope, then string and finally cotton, so that without realising it they were not being supported at all, but were walking. Finally he cut the cotton into pieces so that they could walk around holding the pieces of cotton. They could do it because they thought they could.

> "If you think you'll succeed, you'll succeed. If you think you will fail, you will fail. Either way, you are right."
> Paramahansa Yogananda

According to yoga psychology, mental objects tend to get expressed in the external world. What we think about tends to happen.

This idea is not unique to yoga, nor is it a new discovery. Tribal magic is based on the same principle—hunting parties engaged in rituals enact a successful hunt before embarking on the actual hunt. The shaman painted images of the prey being killed on the cave walls in the belief that if they visualized a kill, it would become real.

In modern sports training, coaches exhort their champions to repeatedly visualize themselves winning, jumping higher, hitting harder, and running faster. In sales and management seminars, managers place great emphasis on the importance of focusing on your goal. Common wisdom proclaims the beneficial effects of positive self-image and mental attitude, and, conversely, the crippling effects of negative thinking. By thinking we are happy, healthy and successful, we tend to become happy, healthy and successful. The reverse is just as true.

The Power of Positive Thinking

Writer Norman Vincent Peale popularized the importance of positive thinking early last century. It has become the basis of motivational and psychological training in business and related fields, utilizing a principle that has been employed in yoga for thousands of years.

Since our thoughts tend to get materialized, our negative ideas also prevent us from manifesting what we want. Our desires fail to achieve their external expression for many reasons, but perhaps the most common is that the negative side of our imagination sabotages our fondest desires. Our imagination has tremendous power; when this power combines with fear or other negative sentiments—doubt, anxiety, worry, insecurity, anger, resentment—they easily nullify all the positive expressions of the will. It is like driving with the handbrake on. Part of us pushes forward while another part restrains us, and the result is a trip to the mechanic.

Meditation teaches us a style of thinking that synchronizes our imagination with our will. We create a positive wave (or mental object) in our mind and then make an effort to focus our attention on it. Whenever negative thought patterns arise and threaten to pull us in a different direction, we redirect our mind back to that positive wave, thereby training ourselves to overcome the distracting, inhibiting influence of the negative thoughts. Through regular practice, this style of thinking becomes a habit and starts affecting other areas of our lives. It is a common experience of regular meditators to have their desires quickly and easily materialized in the external world. However, this is not always a positive experience! Often what we desire is not what is best for our growth and meditators soon learn that they must exercise control over their thoughts and desires for the simple reason that they so often do come true.

Mythology and scriptures are full of stories of people who learned the hard way that getting what you want is not always a good thing. Remember King Midas who, in his greed, wished that all he touched would turn to gold. For a time he enjoyed his newfound wealth, but then his own daughter, returning from a journey, rushed to embrace him. Before he could stop her, she turned into a golden statue.

> "The only thing worse than not getting what you want, is getting what you want."
> Oscar Wilde

While meditation practice has plenty in common with the various schools of positive thinking, there are several crucial differences. Rather than utilizing numerous mental objects (for example, different affirmations) and thereby diffusing our focus, we meditate on one object, which enables us to harness the full power of the mind. And that object is the subtlest object available, Consciousness itself. This leads us to the greatest possible growth and expansion of mind. There is an

we may even become rich or influential, if that is what we really want, but there is no guarantee that even this will bring us lasting happiness.

inherent limitation in a program of positive thinking, if the objective is simply to develop a strong, positive self-image and a sense of well being. We may get all that, we may even become rich or influential, if that is what we really want, but there is no guarantee that even this will bring us lasting happiness.

"People are generally about as happy as they decide to be."
Abraham Lincoln

Mental Power
You were thinking of someone when the phone rang and guess who was on the other end of the phone? You want to go to a concert but can't get a seat; suddenly a friend tells you she has an extra ticket for the show and wonders if you would like it. Has anything like this ever happened to you? Were these coincidences or were they small examples of the powerful connection between thought and physical reality? Meditators everywhere notice a startling increase in the number of such 'coincidences' in their lives after they start meditating. Whether it so happens that meditation speeds up the process by which thoughts are translated into physical reality, or whether it just makes us more aware of our thoughts and how they shape our lives, this phenomenon points directly to the tendency of our mental thoughts to find expression in the external world. How does this happen?

Suppose a desire arises in your mind. That desire activates your imagination. Your mind paints a picture for you of the desired object and you visualize yourself achieving it. Spurred on by the power of that thought-wave, you apply your will power and determination in order to materialize your desire. This driving force—desire, imagination and will power—enables you to translate a thought into reality, though often most or all of this process is unconscious, and all you are aware of is your surprise when your desire 'miraculously' materializes.

Yogis often warn of the dangers of directing the mind towards crude or selfish objectives, particularly when we add the power of concentration to our thinking.

But the opposite can also be true. Many individuals who develop psychic powers through the practice of concentration techniques eventually degenerate because they became deluded by their ego or allow their minds to focus on selfish desires. In his youth, the Yogi Milarepa developed great mental power and used it to avenge wrong done to his family. He later realized how he had allowed himself to degenerate and after undergoing severe spiritual trials, became one of Tibet's greatest Yogis. That is why Yogis often warn of the dangers of directing the mind towards crude or selfish objectives, particularly when we add the power of concentration to our thinking.

Beyond Positive Thinking
"The mind takes the shape of its object."

This old adage of yoga psychology is at the heart of the phenomenon of positive thinking. When you pour water into a container, it will take the shape of the container. Our mind and its thoughts act in a similar way. If you think of a camel, a portion of your mind takes the shape of a camel, or the mind forms an image of a camel. Each and every expression of the universe is vibrational in nature. A thought is a mental wave composed of psychic energy. Because it is vibrational in nature, that mental wave has a particular wavelength. The wavelength of the thought-image of a camel will not be the same as the wavelength of the thought of a vast ocean or a feeling of compassion.

Some thoughts are subtle in character; some are less so. Subtle or expansive thoughts, as you might suspect, have a long, steady wavelength, while crude or mundane thoughts have a much shorter, erratic wavelength. Our mind as a whole has its own characteristic wavelength, which is the composite of all the waves active in the mind at any one time. While our mind's wavelength is constantly changing as different thought-waves rise and fall in our mental ocean, it never changes radically because we each have our own habitual style of thinking—our personality—which determines the nature of the recurring individual thought waves.

What happens when two waves interact? There is clash between the two waves and each is influenced by the other. The stronger the wave, the greater the influence it exerts and the less it is affected by the other wave. When two waves are similar in character, there is very little clash. They vibrate sympathetically. On the practical level we experience this as a natural affinity or dislike for the people and things. Our feeling of 'like' or 'dislike' depends on the degree of sympathetic vibrations between our mental wavelength and that of the object we touch. 'Good vibes' is exactly that, the good vibrations that come when we experience a parallelism between the wavelength of our mind and that of the person or object or environment we encounter.

Exercise—What do You Really Want?
"As you think so you become"

Yoga proverb

96

Before you read this next section, please get out a pen and paper. Ready? OK, Now write down the answer to each question below before you read the next question.

If the mind truly takes on the shape of its object, and we tend to become what we think, we should be careful what we think about. Meditation is not just ordinary thinking; it is concentrated thinking; it amplifies the effects of our thoughts. And when you consider how much time we spend in meditation thinking about one thing, this concept takes on an even greater significance.

1. If you meditate for one hour a day for the rest of your life, how long is that in total?
Of course no one knows how long he or she are going to live. But for every ten more years you live, you'll be spending 3650 hours concentrating on one idea in a universe where thoughts tend to become real.

2. So what are you going to think about? Whatever it is, you are probably going to get it, so choose carefully. What do you want more than anything else in the whole world?
Write it down. Put down this book, and write down what you want more than anything in the whole world.

3. If, upon reflection, your answer seems inadequate, ask yourself this. Why do I want this? Is it in order to get something else? Or is it an end in itself? If it is something else, repeat the question, 'Why do I want this?' Keep repeating the question until you have identified the fundamental desire behind all of your other desires.

Then turn the page.

I've asked this question of hundreds of groups. And I continue to be amazed by the answers. They are all the same. Everyone wants the same thing; and usually it is expressed in one of three words:

Love

Peace

Happiness

4. One more question. How much of this love, peace or happiness do you want?

Let me guess: A little bit? Do you want it to stop—to run out? Are you going to miss feeling unhappy? Do you want your joy to come with an expiration date?

Or do you want the real thing—an eternity of endless bliss?

Endless love, peace and happiness. That's what everyone really wants. All the other things we convince ourselves are important, run after or crave, are really a means to achieve this end state—a state of mind where we always feel perfect happiness, unlimited love, eternal peace. Is this beginning to sound familiar? Isn't this what the great spiritual teachers throughout history have been telling us all along is the ultimate destiny of every individual? Nirvana, Samadhi, Satori, Heavenly Bliss, Enlightenment, Ananda?

Please do not imagine that all those esoteric spiritual teachings have nothing to do with our lives. Nothing could be further from the truth: the message is for us.

So use your allotted hours well. Use them to think about what you really want. This is the way to happiness.

> How much of this love, peace or happiness do you want?

The Ideation of the Mantra

> "A man does not seek to see himself in running water, but in still water. For only what is itself still, can impart stillness unto others."
>
> Chuang-tse

Spiritual meditation can lead us to the blissful domain of our deepest Self, which is the goal of our journey through life. If we want bliss, if we want happiness, if we want freedom, we must meditate on that which is ever blissful, ever happy, and ever free. There is only one place to find this: within ourselves. Our object of meditation is consciousness itself, the infinite source of all things

For a Mantra to be completely effective one must be fully aware of its meaning. Although the simple repetition of your Mantra is helpful, the full benefit can only come if we understand its meaning: 'I am consciousness,' or 'consciousness is all that exists.' All Mantras for meditation have a similar meaning, one that allows us to hold the concept of pure consciousness or pure awareness in our minds as the object of our meditation. Along with this pure awareness comes a feeling. For some, 'consciousness' is too abstract a concept. It has no clear meaning. Think of it as an infinite ocean of love, peace or happiness, bliss or God—whatever resonates closest to our experience. As our meditation progresses, we'll find that it doesn't really make any difference. The ocean of consciousness is an ocean of bliss and love and peace. It is the divine within us. And the essence of the feeling within is that we are dissolving into that ocean, becoming one with it. The waters of the Self are flooding the boundaries of our ego.

> If we want bliss, if we want happiness, if we want freedom, we must meditate on that which is ever blissful, ever happy, and ever free.

It is this feeling which draws us back again and again to our meditation. We feel as if we have come home, and our home is at the very core of our own being. Even a short glimpse of the light of consciousness shining within us is enough to convince us of its reality and to fill us with a yearning to complete our journey.

Try This

• Now that you have some idea of how a Mantra works, you should be able to fully appreciate and enjoy the guided meditation recordings on the included CD. If you're like me, you've probably jumped ahead and listened to it already. No problem, but if not, now is the time.

• Find a peaceful place for your meditation, play the first guided meditation and follow the instructions. Most people find this quite enjoyable, but if you don't find that immediately, don't worry - it will come with practise.

• Now you've come this far you might be ready to start meditating every day. Or twice a day if you want. Use the first recording for your morning meditation, and the second for your evening meditation. Read the tips for meditation in the appendices – these are very helpful.

"It is misleading to think that you are a physical being having a spiritual experience. Rather take the view that you are a spiritual being having a worldly experience."
Teilhard de Chardin

Chapter Six

Ego and Intuition

"The Cosmos is a bedlam of noisy confusion. Everything in it is subjected to a constant bombardment by millions of conflicting electromagnetic and sound waves. Life protects itself from this turmoil by using sense organs, which are like narrow slits, letting in only a very limited range of frequencies. But sometimes even these are too much, so there is the additional barrier of the nervous system, which filters the input and sorts it out into 'useful information' and 'irrelevant noise...' We all have this ability to focus on certain stimuli and to ignore others. A good example is 'cocktail party concentration,' which enables us to tune in to the sound of just one person's voice among so many, all saying similar things...Living organisms select information from their surroundings, process it according to a program (in this case one that will ensure the best possible chance of survival), and supply an output of order (which is in turn a source of raw materials and information for other life)."

From Supernature by Lyall Watson

According to both Western and yoga psychology the mind is composed of several layers. Most people are familiar with the modern Western analysis of the mind as three layers: conscious, subconscious and unconscious. Yoga psychology goes a step further and divides the mind into five layers: the first two roughly correspond to the conscious and subconscious minds of Western psychology; the remaining three layers are sections of the unconscious, or superconscious mind and include what Jung referred to as the collective unconscious.

Both psychological models theorize that the outer layers of the mind are mainly responsible for our interactions with physical or external reality, while the inner layers are primarily concerned with subtler internal realities. Yoga psychology regards the physical body with its central nervous system as the outermost layer of the mind. It is here that information related to our survival is processed and it is here also that much of our conditioning is stored or expressed. Patterns created by past experiences are imprinted in our nervous system; many of our responses to external stimuli are determined by the patterns encoded there.

The controller of our conscious physical actions is the ego. 'Ego' in Latin means 'I.' It is the ego, which we ordinarily think of as our 'self.' The western division of the mind into Id, Ego and superego essentially refers to the functions of the ego. The ego processes the information received by the senses and translates our thoughts into actions. Though human beings have instincts like all other living organisms, most of our activity is controlled and directed by the ego. Without it we would all die; it is the source of our intelligence and it compels us to act in order to survive.

According to yoga psychology, the fundamental quality that sustains the ego is the sense of doer-ship. Ego is the feeling 'I am doing' or 'I am the doer.' It can make you feel so involved in an activity that you do not feel any clear distinction between your sense of 'I' and your action. 'I am going to the shop, I am eating, I feel happy, I feel sad.

> "...it is primarily upon the activating capacity of the ego that the process of physical activity depends. It is also on this activating (radiating) capacity of a person that their personality depends. The more developed the radiating power, the more shining will be the personality."
> Shrii Shrii Anandamurti

Our ego-self has its limitations—and its special gifts. It clearly has an indispensable role to play in the life of a human being. Without the ego we could not function in the world: we need it to get to work in the morning and to home at night. Someone has to drive the car and pay attention to the traffic lights! With the ego's capacity for rational thinking, flights of imagination along with its determination and willpower, it is able to act in the world and bring desire to fruition. The more clearly it thinks, the greater its imaginative powers and the stronger its will power, the more we are able to accomplish with succinct control in our lives. Every success story contains a strong, developed ego. Just as we need to strengthen our bodies through diet and exercise, we need to fortify this ego, which manages all the mundane aspects of our existence and enables us to achieve what we strive for in the world.

Meditation is not about neglecting our bodies or negating our ego-self. Rather, its purpose is to develop and strengthen all the layers of our mind.

> The ego is only the visible portion of the iceberg that is the Self, and to remain oblivious to the far greater submerged part is as dangerous for us as it was for the Titanic on its ill-fated crossing of the Atlantic.

Meditation is not about neglecting our bodies or negating our ego-self. Rather, its purpose is to develop and strengthen all the layers of our mind. The stronger the various layers are, the easier it will be for us to cross the boundaries of the ego-self to reach the vastness of our Greater Self. Regular meditation strengthens our ego by building our capacity to control our mind and direct it towards a goal. As we develop this ability, we feel its effects in every area of our life. We are able to focus more clearly on our goals and to pursue them with increased determination and mental stamina. Experienced meditators share the feeling anything is achievable with correct mental focus.

The ego is only the visible portion of the iceberg that is the Self, and to remain oblivious to the far greater submerged part is as dangerous for us as it was for the Titanic on its ill-fated crossing of the Atlantic.

> *"To the egotist He says, 'you are but a little spark and yet you extol yourself so much. I own the whole universe, but I remain silent in the background.'"*
>
> Paramahansa Yogananda

How can the ego trap us? Let us count the ways...

Faulty Programming

> *"Life is a bundle of misunderstandings."*
>
> Avt. Ananda Bharati Ac.

Our interpretation of what happens to us in our daily life is generally determined more by our perspective than by the actual events. Physicists tell us that what is 'really' happening in the physical world is: a host of sub-atomic particles fly around at incredible speeds in the middle of a great void, and these particles themselves are just wave forms or energy within the mysterious fabric of space-time. However, we don't see any of this, and our experience of reality varies greatly according to our mother tongue, conceptual framework, upbringing, biases and conditioning. They are the colored spectacles through which we view this whirling dance of atomic particles.

If we are to understand anything—or even survive—we require these spectacles to protect our eyes and enable us to interpret what we see. Every day we are bombarded by thousands of different experiences and impressions. Often we need to make instantaneous decisions. Time is short, so we each build up our own data bank of 'pre-judgments,' which enable us to make an instantaneous response upon demand. These 'pre-judices' based on past experience get handed to us by our family, friends and social institutions. They shape our personality and condition the way we react to our environment. But sometimes the programming goes wrong. If there is a faulty input at one end we misread reality.

Here's a story from my friend Declan:

A 13 year old boy named Ramesh came to live with me in our meditation center in Auckland, New Zealand. Ramesh was part Maori, very courageous and intelligent. One morning I was busy planning the day's activities with my colleagues and preparing some papers for an appointment I had later in the day. When it was time to leave I picked up the phone to make some urgent calls but Ramesh was on the line. I must have picked up the receiver a dozen times over the next few minutes but he was still on the line. His little brother was visiting and I was sure they were plotting something together.

"Will you youngsters get off the phone," I shouted. "I need to make a few calls before I go out!"

"Can't, this is important," Ramesh shouted back.

"What is it that's so important?" I demanded.

"Can't say," came the reply.

"Right, you guys are obviously up to some mischief again," I said impatiently. Finally I insisted that they hang up so I could make my calls and leave. As I was driving down the road with the radio on, I began thinking angrily: "Young people are so selfish. You try your level best to help them out and what do you get? Nothing but trouble!"

Just then, my favorite song came on the radio, a winsome ballad by the Irish folk-singer, Mary Black. I felt my anger melting away as I listened to the captivating sound of her voice. I remembered telling Ramesh that it was my favorite song and now, because my mood had changed, I felt embarrassed about the way I had been thinking about him. He was, after all, only a kid. It was his business to be full of energy and up to mischief. The song ended and the disc jockey announced: "That was a special request for Declan from Ramesh." The boys had been calling the radio station to ask them to play a song for me!

This next incident reportedly occurred in Ireland.

A man was working in the post office sorting Christmas letters. A letter arrived addressed to Santa at the North Pole. He opened it and read:

Dear Santa,

I am a widow with a seven-year-old son. I am on a pension and can't afford to get him the gift he wants for Christmas. I need another twenty-five pounds. Please send it soon. I have every confidence in you, Santa.

Yours sincerely

Mrs. Mary Aherne

10a McDougal Grove,

MacBride

County Cork

The man was so moved by the letter that he organized a collection with a hat and collected fifteen pounds, which he mailed to the lady, from 'Santa.' A few weeks later he received another letter to Santa from the same lady:

Dear Santa,

I received your letter with the money inside. I am sorry to mention this, but that toy my little boy had his heart set on costs, as I mentioned, twenty-five pounds. Unfortunately, I only received fifteen pounds in your letter. But then you know how they are at the post office.

Yours sincerely,

Mrs. Mary Aherne

Gurdjieff once said that before someone can break out of a cage, they must first realize they are in the cage. To the extent that we identify with our conditioning, biases and preconceptions, they become the walls of a prison that we cannot see. We become stuck in ways of looking at and dealing with the world that often brings only misery to ourselves and others. Before we can break free, we must recognise the walls of that prison for what they are. Meditation aids this process. As we develop our conscious awareness of the preconceptions that distort our perspective, we also become capable of seeing what is important and what isn't. Then we can keep the best and discard the rest.

> before someone can break out of a cage, they must first realize they are in the cage.

Off Course

It seems that in modern society we are trying to live our lives back to front. We are encouraged to own things, to do more things we like in

> First you have to find out who you are; then you will know what you need to do, and have a clearer idea of what you really want.

order to become happier. But, in fact, it works better the other way around. First you have to find out who you are; then you will know what you need to do, and have a clearer idea of what you really want.

This back to front approach to happiness is imposed, whether through coercion or through a system of incentives, on the whole of society by the wealthy and powerful. At the beginning of the Industrial Revolution in Europe and America—and still in the developing world today—people worked long hours at physically demanding tasks. The living conditions of coal miners and factory workers were only slightly better than that of the mules working beside them. Their physical bodies could not take the pressure of such arduous labour, and disease and mortality rates increased dramatically.

In the modern business world, people expend huge amounts of mental energy in the race to get ahead and be successful. The demand for intense mental work in the pursuit of the goals of modern business exhausts the mind and nervous system, resulting in many casualties. For every jet setter who succeeds in keeping up the pace, hundreds fail. Through the ranks of slickly attired executives exuding false confidence creeps an epidemic of stress related illnesses, nervous breakdowns, alcoholism, broken families and broken dreams. For many of these people their lives have become a gilded cage; their egos yoked like 'bullocks to the grinding-wheels of commerce.' They struggle to cope, but the pressures of modern living leave them with no time to care for their emotional and spiritual needs. And we're only discussing the condition of the 'lucky' elite of this modern system.

> *"Poor slave*
> *They took the shackles from your body*
> *And put the shackles on your mind"*
> Traditional song from the black slave days in America

Our willpower, the drive within us to manifest our dreams in physical form, has enormous potential; like our bodies, our willpower, if used wisely, helps us to progress in every aspect of our lives. However, when we overexert our will things may start to fall apart; we may fall, from being extremely dynamic to profoundly lethargic.

A highly qualified chartered accountant managed an institution with a staff of more than 2,000 people. He had been made redundant, lost his job and, due to his advancing age, failed to find a similar position to match his qualifications. This dynamic, charming and intelligent man suddenly felt listless, directionless and had to force himself to keep active.

Our emotional life needs energy. Our spiritual life needs energy and radiating power. Your body can keep your spirit and mind firmly planted on the ground. Your willpower has the capacity to make the earth a heaven for you. But if your ego is tied to the yoke of modern materialistic society, your spirit will not go anywhere except to the bank, the shrink or the undertaker.

Modern life places too many demands on the ego, and our entire being suffers for it. The ego, which controls the body and manifests our desires, receives more and more pressure to perform, to make things happen, or to produce—things to sit on, drive to the office, eat or drink or wear. But like the body, the ego also grows tired from overwork. It will break down and then frustration sets in. Even worse, we are told that our ego is all there is and we believe it. We think there is no escape from the frustration. Society has left us to 'toil at the wheel' because they made us believe that is all there is to life.

> *"...it is only since the end of the nineteenth century that modern psychology, with its inductive methods, has discovered the foundations of consciousness and proved empirically the existence of a psyche outside consciousness. With this discovery the position of the ego, 'til then absolute, became relativised; that is to say, though it retains its quality as the center of the field of consciousness, it is questionable whether it is the center of the personality. It is part of the personality but not the whole of it."*
>
> Carl Gustav Jung

I did it

How often do we push ourselves to accomplish something only in order to impress other people? The emotional satisfaction we get from feeling we are 'somebody,' in someone else's eyes, is often more important to us than the accomplishment itself. But when our self-respect depends on the opinions of others, it becomes a trap as hard as a steel cage.

> *"Tell me how a person gets their respect and I will tell you who they are."*
>
> Dale Carnegie

"The intelligent man who is proud of his intelligence is like a condemned man who is proud of his large cell."
Simone Weil

Of all of our travels, the one with the least prospect of a happy ending is the 'ego trip.' Everybody tries to pretend, to put on a face, a mask, in order to impress everybody else, as if we were all participants in a masquerade ball. Yet the very people we are trying to impress are busy trying to impress us! In the end nobody is fooled, nobody is impressed, and we are left alone holding an empty mask on a stick.

Each of us is unique and special, but our true uniqueness and beauty do not lie in the trappings of the ego. What is lasting and of greatest value in our lives lies beyond the conscious mind. This is the uniqueness that we all share but too few of us realize.

> Of all of our travels, the one with the least prospect of a happy ending is the 'ego trip.'

Beyond the Conscious Mind

"I am too old and too lazy to write poems.
Age seems to be my only loyal friend now.
In some life long ago I was (unfortunately) a poet.
Perhaps I was a painter (or some sort of painter) too.
As is customary, the world remembers me
For this or that movement of my hand.
My name is known because this hand moves thus.
But the real me, ah!
That they cannot reach."
Wang Wei

The ego is restricted to the realm of 'doing and having' where 'having' is just another form of 'doing.' People become trapped in this continuous feeling of doing and never realize that the greater part of themselves lies beyond the ego, beyond the feeling of 'doing and having.'

"The purpose of meditation, paradoxically, is to learn to simply 'be.' Since nearly everything we do in life is done with some goal in mind, most of our actions are only the means to an end, pointing us continually toward a future that does not exist. But meditation, when no goal disturbs it, allows us to

discover the richness and profundity of the present moment. We begin to realize the miraculous power of our own lives— not as they will be, or as we might imagine they once were at some golden time in the past, but as they actually are. Meditation is one of the few things in life that is not about DOING but about BEING.'"

Rick Fields

Many people catch a glimpse of a pure sense of awareness, a sense of pure existence. It might have been during a quiet moment by the seashore or while listening to a beautiful piece of music. Such experiences come when our minds momentarily let go of our agendas and motives, our preoccupations and desires. When this happens, most of us don't really know how we got there, but for that one moment everything just 'is' and it seems perfect.

> **Many people catch a glimpse of a pure sense of awareness, a sense of pure existence.**

Some years ago I was staying at Ananda Nagar, a spiritual community in India. Walking alone one afternoon along a path through the fields, I found myself filled by a sense of the most perfect peace imaginable. There seemed to be no need to ever worry about anything again. I desired nothing; I never felt more content. This sublime feeling remained to some degree for several hours. I do not know why it came. I do not know why it went.

It is important to remember that this kind of experience should not be confused with 'enlightenment' or 'Self-Realization.' Such experiences may be profound and meaningful, but they are just glimpses of the spiritual reality, and can as well occur at the beginning of the spiritual path, as near its end. As long as there is any feeling of ego at all, any sense of separation from Cosmic Consciousness, then we still have some distance to go.

The ego is the part of the mind that keeps us from enjoying this sublime level of consciousness as our natural state. The constant movement of thought, the incessant coming and going, acts as a veil between us and this quiet joyful awareness. If the veil is thick enough, if our identification with the ego is complete, we don't even realize that there is something more—a state of mind more profound and satisfying than anything ever experienced. This is how the ego becomes our prison with bars between us and our experience of our inner Self.

A man was interested in Zen Buddhism. He studied philosophy for some years and approached a famous Zen Master for instruction. He started telling the master all he knew about philosophy and what he understood to be the meaning of existence. After he had spoken for some time, he paused for breath. The master said, "Would you like a cup of tea?"

The aspirant was surprised, as he expected the master to respond to his erudite philosophical exposition with some words of wisdom. Out of politeness he replied, "Yes, thank you."

The master proceeded to prepare and pour the tea in silence, and the aspirant went on talking about how much he knew until he noticed that the master was continuing to pour the tea into his cup after it was full and overflowing. Then the hot tea spilled off the table onto his lap. He jumped up with an exclamation. "How can you be so careless! You are still pouring tea when there is no more room in the cup!"

The master smiled. "That is correct. There is no more room. Your cup is full."

> "Discovery takes place, not when the mind is crowded with knowledge, but when knowledge is absent; only then is there stillness and space, and in this state understanding or discovery comes into being. Knowledge is undoubtedly useful at one level, but at another it is positively harmful."
> Krishnamurti

In order to receive wisdom, we have to forget how much we think we know. We have to re-discover what the Zen Buddhists call 'Beginner's Mind.' Before any more water can be added, we learn how to empty our cup. We let go of the things we do as habit, the things we think we know, the beliefs and judgments we have, and go into the 'I' at the root of all these expressions of the ego.

The part of us which is beyond the realm of doing/owning exists in our pure sense of existence, in the feeling of 'I.' We all know the experience of 'I am doing the laundry.' What we miss is the part of us that is behind the doing. The 'I am doing' is forever changing. 'I am happy' turns into 'I am sad' and the 'I am sad' decides to get up off the couch and take out the laundry. But the 'I' that experiences these various conditions is constant. The same sense of existence lies hidden at the root of every one of the little actions that string themselves together to make up the continuum of our life. It is the one constant in our life.

This 'I' feeling is also the one constant among all of the Individuals—

> This 'I' feeling is also the one constant among all of the Individuals-the one thing that we all share.

the one thing that we all share. Remember the many moons reflected in the cow's footprints? Our individual 'I' feelings are just miniature reflections of the Universal Consciousness, or Paramatman—the Supreme Soul, or God.

Meditation teaches us how to get to that 'I' by training us to go beyond all the mental activity that keeps us away from it. We have all experienced being caught up in a situation or an emotion and suddenly, for one fleeting moment, we mentally step back, and watch ourselves as we might watch a fish floundering in a net. But the moment passes because we have not learned to break the bonds of our identification with the doer of the action, or our sense of ego. We can only release that chain of identification when we quiet the activities of the ego, and when we enter a state of stillness where there is no place for the ego. The ego has a natural fear of its own dissolution. We fear that if we stop being so busy doing or having, we will stop being. But the opposite is true. It is only when the ego bows out for a time, when we stop identifying with our actions, achievements and possessions, that we become fully aware of our own existence.

Descartes based his famous proof of existence on the statement 'I think, therefore I am,' and this concept lies at the heart of the Western view of life. This limited view fails to acknowledge the presence of a deeper self behind the thinking. It is possible to realize through meditation that we are not our thoughts. Our true self is the unchanging awareness of existence located at the core of our being.

Intuition

> *"You must merge the 'I do' feeling with your existential 'I' feeling. This is how human beings establish themselves in the realm of intuition."*
>
> Shrii Shrii Anandamurti

Intuition is the name we give to those faculties of mind that lie beyond the domain of the ego, outside the realms of what we think of as the conscious and subconscious minds. When an insight or fragment of information trickles down from the level of pure transcendental awareness into our waking consciousness, we find ourselves having knowledge and experiences that the rational mind cannot account for.

At the age of sixteen I dreamed that my best friend five hundred miles away had a car accident on a particular road. I found out the next day that he had in fact had an accident on that very road.

Perhaps you have experienced knowing what someone was going to say just before they said it, or who is calling before you even pick up the phone. Perhaps you and a friend have found you were both humming the same tune in your heads or you might have racked your brains trying to solve a difficult problem, only to find that the solution came to you in a sudden flash some time later.

These are all tiny instances of what we call intuition, sparks of knowledge that cannot logically be explained by our narrow, ego-bound view of the world. Mystics, throughout history and from widely different cultures, report experiences of communion with a mysterious, limitless intelligence that pervades all of existence, an infinite awareness that connects us all, whether or not we are conscious of it. Their accounts provide us with a record of the possibilities of human experience that cannot be ignored.

> Intuition is the name we give to those faculties of mind that lie beyond the domain of the ego, outside the realms of what we think of as the conscious and subconscious minds.

"...Whatever the place or period in which they have arisen, their aims, doctrines, and methods have been substantially the same. Their experiences, therefore, form a body of evidence, curiously consistent and often mutually explanatory, which must be taken into account before we can add up the sum of the energies and potentialities of the human spirit or reasonably speculate on its relation to the unknown world, which lies beyond the boundaries of the senses."

Evelyn Underhill

One of the experiences common to all of these explorers of inner space: all of life is interconnected because all of life partakes of the same consciousness, which is, in fact, the substratum of existence. Consciousness is one, they insist, but we fail to experience this because we are blinded to the deeper experiences of existence by the veils of our ego. Yet, if we look around us, examples of the interconnectedness

> Consciousness is one, they insist, but we fail to experience this because we are blinded to the deeper experiences of existence by the veils of our ego.

of life are everywhere. In his popular book Supernature, Lyall Watson describes a somewhat horrific experiment done in Russia in the 1960s:

Researchers took newly born rabbits to the depths of the sea in a submarine and kept the mother ashore in a laboratory with electrodes implanted deep in her brain. At intervals, the rabbits in the submarine were killed one by one, and at the precise moment that each of her offspring died there were sharp electrical responses in the brain waves of the mother. There is no known physical way that a submerged submarine can communicate with anyone on land, and yet even rabbits seem to be able to make contact in a moment of crisis.

For years naturalists were unable to understand how birds flying in formation were suddenly able to change direction all together. After analysing hours of film they failed to find a single instance of one bird moving first. The birds all changed direction at exactly the same moment with no scientifically plausible explanation for how they communicated their intentions to each other.

Cambridge scientist Dr Rupert Sheldrake writes in 'Seven Experiments that will Change the World' of a dog that was filmed waiting by the door in anticipation when its mistress decided to return home from the far side of the city at an unscheduled time. These experiments were repeated on numerous occasions, effectively proving the existence of some sort of extra-sensory communication between dogs and humans.

Numerous examples of this telepathic communication exist among other species. Human beings are no exception. Curiously, telepathy is far more common among indigenous peoples than among people living a more modern lifestyle. Perhaps this suggests that the dominating and overworked intellect and associated ego of modern peoples erect a barrier between us and our intuition.

C. G. Jung is the western thinker most credited with having explored the subtler psychic realities and those mysterious areas of consciousness that lie beyond the ego.

> telepathy is far more common among indigenous peoples than among people living a more modern lifestyle.

Among his many discoveries was the existence of what he called the 'collective unconscious,' a vast, transpersonal storehouse of knowledge common to us all. He found that his patients, while drawing images from their dreams, were tapping into the past experience of all mankind to draw symbols from other times and other cultures, symbols that they could not possibly have come across in their personal lives. He found these symbols to be ways of describing the deeper, transpersonal elements of our psychic existence in the language of the conscious mind.

> *"A symbol is a mythological sign that has one leg here and the other in infinity. It points to the transcendent."*
> C. G. Jung

Developing Intuition

> Ego has its place, which is that of a faithful servant ready to do the bidding of its master, Consciousness.

How do we develop this intuition? How can we gain access to the vast reaches of the mind that lie concealed by the restless activities of the ego? The secret lies in our 'I' feeling, our pure sense of existence. The next time you find yourself caught up in a situation, try to step back for a moment and get in touch with the 'I' that is taking part in the drama. 'I am so angry...I've got to finish this on time...' Focus on the 'I' instead. Watch it as if you were a spectator and not an actor on the stage. It is not easy, but we all have the capacity to do it, once we can shift our attention away from the drama. The moment we think of our 'I' and make the effort to concentrate our attention there, we have begun to step back into mindfulness, our awareness of self. Your inner 'I' is there at the core of everything you do. You only have to pay attention to it to start identifying with who you really are, and not with all the comings and goings of this relative, physical world.

The problem comes when the ego butts in and demands our full attention.

Ego has its place, which is that of a faithful servant ready to do the bidding of its master, Consciousness. But it doesn't know its place—it insists on being the center of attention like a spoiled child. And just like a child, we must treat it firmly but lovingly. We must teach it how to behave. That's where meditation comes in. Meditation is there to teach the ego how to behave and to help us understand who we really are. When we sit down to meditate, the ego is still active. We have thoughts, desires, and preoccupations. But during meditation we train our mind to concentrate on consciousness, on the pure awareness which is the source from which all these thoughts arise. As we redirect our mind inwards, we become aware of the thoughts that pull us away from our object of concentration. We see the mind in action, the complexes, anxieties, desires and mad rush of the ego towards its fulfilment in the physical world. But because we are meditating on consciousness we become ever more aware of ourselves as the spectator. The thoughts become the background; the still place at the center becomes the foreground and the place from where we sit and watch. Gradually these thoughts subside like foam in the wake of a departing wave. The inexorable joy of that quiescent awareness pulls us deeper and deeper inside, until all we find is ocean, the ocean of 'I,' the ocean of our deepest self. When emerge from meditation we retain that experience.

> The thoughts become the background; the still place at the center becomes the foreground and the place from where we sit and watch. Gradually these thoughts subside like foam in the wake of a departing wave.

My meditation students sometimes complain that meditation is too simple. There has got to be more to it, they say. They want more to think about, visualize, feel. It is too hard to try to think of only one thing. That's actually the point and the beauty of it! It is simple and hard at the same time. Thinking and visualizing are familiar functions of the mind. We use them as springboards in the process of our meditation but eventually we must leave them behind to venture into the unknown. Our duty is to stop thinking and start being. Meditation gives the mind the bare minimum of ideas to focus on as a stepping-stone to the state of pure awareness.

Try This

•Find a quiet spot for meditation. Get settled, close your eyes and watch your breathing for a while. Now mentally ask yourself the question: Who am I? Pause for a while, and ask yourself again, mentally, Who am I? Keep doing this for ten minutes.

•Write down your observations in your journal.

•This exercise is not a substitute for your daily, or twice daily, mantra meditation. The purpose of this exercise, which I suggest you try at least two or three times, is just to help you develop a deeper sense of your inner consciousness.

"I said to my soul, be still,
And let the dark come upon you
Which shall be the darkness of God.
As, in a theatre,
The lights are extinguished,
For the scene to be changed
With a hollow rumble of wings,
With a movement of darkness on darkness,
And we know that the hills and the trees,
The distant panorama
And the bold imposing façade
Are all being rolled away
I said to my soul, be still,
And wait without hope
For hope would be hope of the wrong thing;
Wait without love
For love would be love of the wrong thing
There is yet faith
But the faith and the love and the hope
Are all in the waiting.
Wait without thought
For you are not ready of thought;
So the darkness shall be the light,
And the stillness, the dancing."
                                        T.S. Eliot

Chapter Seven

Karma: Be Yourself-
Everyone Else is Taken

"I cannot believe that God plays dice with the Universe."
Albert Einstein.

The chance that this immeasurably vast, incredibly intricate universe was created and maintained by accident is akin to the odds of a gale blowing through a junkyard, scattering thousands of scraps of metal, and assembling in its wake a jumbo jet. Not simply unlikely, but for all practical purposes impossible.

Humans have always suspected that there is a mysterious intelligence behind this creation. We are conscious beings in a world inconceivably more complex than anything we could ever create with the limited intelligence of our individual minds. We may not agree on the answer to it all, but most of us sense a hidden mystery, beyond our comprehension. Who or what it is, we are not quite sure, but who would not like to find out?

> *"You have come with the tremor of winter*
> *Who are you? What is this beauty of yours?*
> *Covering the green fields with ice and snow*
> *Who are you? What is this beauty of yours?*
> *In the biting north wind*
> *On the leafless trees by the wayside*
> *You wrote an unknown message."*
>
> *Prabhat Samgiita, song no. 94*
> P.R. Sarkar.

Despite our lingering feeling that the ultimate truth is a mystery that constantly escapes us, we know that it expresses itself in ways that we can see and feel due to its impact on our lives. There are universal laws that govern our existence, inescapable because they are woven into the very fabric of the universe. The law of gravity keeps our feet firmly anchored to the planet as we walk; archetypal polarity is reflected in every facet of existence: night and day, birth and death, man and woman, yin and yang. One of the most subtle of these universal laws— but one that is far-reaching in its consequences—is the law of cause and effect, that of Karma: every action creates a reaction, and hidden behind every action is a cause.

This eternal chain of action and reaction is like a string of dominoes. One domino tumbles after being struck by the one behind it, and it in turn sends the next one tumbling. Along the way it is easy to lose sight of all the dominoes that have gone before, but they are important nonetheless, each playing its indispensable role in determining the outcome of the entire chain. Some of these dominoes are made of molecules and sub-atomic particles, while others are thought-waves. Together, this intricate dance of particles and waves makes up the bowl of quantum soup we call the Universe. Sometimes a thought-domino bumps a molecule-domino; at other times it's the molecule-domino that bumps the thought-domino. It is always just one more bump in a vast chain of cause and effect.

Let us say we decide to make a chair. From the scientific perspective of modern physics, a chair is composed mainly of empty space and contains billions of tiny electrical charges and atomic and sub-atomic particles, all flying around in some orderly fashion. The same is true of the wood in the chair. Now we come along and take that piece of wood and carve it and sand it and paint it. We stand back and admire our handiwork, glowing with satisfaction because we created something new. But did we really? Did we create the molecules that comprise that piece of wood? Did we create the flesh and blood in our hands that enabled us to carry out our work?

Try to peer down that long corridor of actions and reactions. What was it that caused us to perceive this gyrating kaleidoscope of molecules as a 'chair?' Might it be due to certain 'pre-judgments' arising from past experience and conditioning? Can we even be sure that the original thought, the desire to make the chair, was in fact an original thought? Could it also have a cause? Might it also not be a reaction to something else, a single domino tumbling in a sweep of dominoes? Might it not be that subconsciously we wanted to make the chair in order to impress the people around us or to prove something to our parents or to fulfil some long-hidden need, and that each of these previous desires or psychic reactions arose out of other conditions that led to them?

Twentieth-century physics, more than anything else, has engraved this understanding so indelibly in the modern mind. Quantum theory demonstrates that all things appear to be connected, and even suggests that mere observation of a phenomenon changes the nature of that phenomenon. The limitations of Newtonian physics, that the world is composed of solid objects and empty space, were delineated long ago, prompting such responses as the celebrated statement of the English Astronomer, Sir James Jeans, that 'the world looks more and more like a giant thought than a giant machine.'

"One leaf, fluttering,
Tells of autumn
Over all the country."

A Zen Forest: Sayings of the Masters

The intricacies of the law of cause and effect are too great to be easily understood, let alone the vast mystery from which it arises, so throughout history we have turned to men and women of wisdom for explanations—to people of science, philosophy, psychology and, most of all, religion.

As ye Sow, so Shall ye Reap

Religions always delve into the ultimate mysteries of life. Priests and theologians try, with decreasing success, to retain this field as their private domain. Nevertheless, no exploration of the ultimate mysteries is complete without an examination of the religious view of these matters.

Every scripture describes a divine or cosmic law governing the consequences of our actions. Many of us intuitively feel its existence without ever attending a single lecture or perusing through the pages of whatever thick black book presides over the religion of our childhoods. Isn't it natural that something bad results from harmful actions? It may not keep us from doing those 'bad' things, but the voice of our conscience creates a 'gut-feeling' when we do something wrong.

Different religions use this teaching in various ways: as a caution against sin, or even as a clever means of manipulation or exploitation. People tend to find a way to escape negative consequences of our actions.

Historically, the priest class, claiming the power of intercession, took advantage of this tendency. For a small donation, they promised to fix things with the Big Guy upstairs in control of actions and reactions. They further consolidated their position by preying on people's fear of the consequences of their actions. Ancient and medieval theological literature is replete with grim descriptions of the torments of the underworld—what a picturesque but frightening way to draw people's attention to the law of Karma. These

> Most people understand that no one, no matter how well-placed they may be or how much money we give them, can change the laws of the universe to escape what is coming to them.

medieval concepts are not confined to the past. A colleague was asked what he did for a living. When he replied that he taught meditation, the man looked serious and said, "You'd better shape up, son. Hell's going to be hot for you."

Few people still believe today that another human being can possess the power to intercede for them with the Cosmic Command Post. Most people understand that no one, no matter how well-placed they may be or how much money we give them, can change the laws of the universe to escape what is coming to them. For better or for worse, we are stuck with the consequences of what we do.

Don't Complain. It's God's Will

A second, common teaching of many religious schools and doctrines is the passive acceptance of the law of Karma; a kind of fatalism which leads people to believe that because everything is the will of God, they need not change the way things are. I personally believe this kind of thinking propagated during the European Middle Ages to legitimatize the oppressive rule by the rich overlords and keep the serfs in their place. Such thinking is still widespread in India today as part of the Hindu religious belief. Brahmin priests justify the suffering of the poor, arguing that it is a result of the sins of their past lives.

This misinterpretation of the law of Karma, sometimes deliberate, is not even logical. If it is God's will for someone to be poor, and you are in a position to help them, it could equally be God's will for you to exercise your God-given faculty of compassion and help them. Surely this is more likely than the alternative proposition that a supposedly loving God created this situation in order to demonstrate that you have a heart of stone.

If we are the ones suffering, perhaps we have the right to adopt a philosophical attitude and accept it as a consequence of our own past misdeeds. But to presume to interpret the cause of someone else's suffering, and then use it as an excuse to neglect or oppress them, is hardly a humane, let alone a spiritual, attitude.

> We may trust in the wisdom of a divine intelligence, but we should at the same time endeavour to make the best possible use of whatever intelligence and energy given to us.

It may well be that everything is the will of God, but does that mean we should not get out of bed in the morning? Or breathe or eat? Even the decision to do nothing is a decision like any other, and carries with it a set of consequences, the same as if we had decided instead to go out and try to save the world, or to sit in meditation and make an effort to master our minds. No matter what we do or don't do, we cannot escape the chain of cause and effect. The mere fact that we are breathing and eating to keep our body alive means that we are consuming the earth's resources. We are involved in a chain of cause and effect that affects not only ourselves, but all the living beings on the planet. We may trust in the wisdom of a divine intelligence, but we should at the same time endeavour to make the best possible use of whatever intelligence and energy given to us.

> *"Trust in Allah, but tie your camel."*
> Sufi proverb

The easy answers of organized religion often fail to satisfy that thirst for understanding. We sense that the causes behind our difficulties and concerns lie buried in our own past, hidden behind a dark curtain. The desire to understand the forces that shape our individual destiny fuelled the great upsurge of psychology and psychological research of the twentieth century and opened the way for the huge influence it now exerts over perceptions of ourselves. Are psychologists the new priesthood?

From the Mind's Eye

Psychologists are the first to agree that everything in the world is subject to the law of action and reaction, but they encourage us to not waste time worrying about the workings of a divine intelligence since everything relating to Karma is already present in our own minds. Too much is beyond our control—whether it is an earthquake or China invading India, who can predict what will happen? Can we realistically expect to understand the workings of a universe that is beyond our powers of comprehension? An event here might have an effect on Mars, as the physicists say, but will we even be aware of it?

When we go to an automatic teller machine at the bank, we plug into a central computer system that coordinates the resources of millions of accounts all over the country. The amount of information that passes through that computer system in one day is staggering, simply beyond our comprehension. But need we worry about it? All we really care about is the money we've come to withdraw. That's what concerns us.

That central computer system is like the universal intelligence, which ultimately decides whether or not we get our $20 and a chance to spend another Saturday night at the movies. It's a vast operation, handling the daily transactions of millions of accounts, but fortunately all we have to concern ourselves with is our own individual account. We have our personal banking card and this gives us access to our own funds. As long as we have something in our account, we can get it out at any hour of the day or night.

In the same way, what concerns modern psychology most about the law of cause and effect is how our past actions and experiences shape our personality. Whatever your individual destiny, whether you are an alcoholic, a perfect mother, a delinquent teenager or the Pope, this has come about as a result of reactions to past actions and experiences stretching back as far as your early childhood, all stored in your mind. The mind houses the impressions of the events shaping our lives and these impressions have give rise to the reactions that create your unique personal situation in the world today. The key to understanding who we are lies in understanding what impressions are stored in our minds, especially those which have become unconscious; just as the key to figuring out if you can get the $20 you want lies in punching in the pin number of your bank card and verifying that you have enough money in your account.

> *"What we are now is the result of whatever we have done or thought in the past; and whatever we shall be in the future will be the result of what we do or think now."*
> Swami Vivekananda

Yoga Psychology

Thousands of years ago practitioners of meditation formulated the law of Karma based on their observations of both the human mind and the external world. The law of Karma says that for every action there is a reaction. Newton discovered this in relation to the laws governing the physical world back in the Eighteenth Century, but the law of Karma applies the same idea to the realm of the mind. Thoughts produce reactions, as surely and as consistently as a falling ball bounces up again.

However: these reactions to psychic

> Thoughts produce reactions, as surely and as consistently as a falling ball bounces up again.

actions are not always immediate. The reactions are usually stored in the mind as impressions waiting for the right conditions for their release.

If you poke your finger in a rubber ball and pull it out again the ball will immediately spring back to its original shape. There is a reactive force within the material structure of the ball, which opposes your action and wants to regain its original state. But if you leave your finger in the ball, the conditions necessary for it to express that reaction will not be present. You will have to remove your finger before the ball can regain its original shape.

> A key point to remember about Karma is that it is not, strictly speaking, the action or experience which creates the lasting impression, but our mental reaction to it.

The mind functions in much the same way. Any psychic action, whether or not it is expressed in the material world, creates a distortion in our mind-stuff (or ectoplasm). Our thoughts have momentum, as does any wave, and this momentum leaves an impression in our mind, similar to a wave leaving an impression on the sand at the edge of the sea. As long as that impression is not released through a reaction, the impression will remain, conditioning our mind and how it expresses itself. The deeper the impression, the greater influence it will have over our mental makeup—and the more forcefully it will express itself when it is finally released. A key point to remember about Karma is that it is not, strictly speaking, the action or experience which creates the lasting impression, but our mental reaction to it. It is not so much what happens or what we do, but what we think that matters. Of course, our actions are direct or indirect reflections of our thoughts. Two people commit a nearly identical act of violence, but one person feels remorse even while committing that act and afterwards vows to himself never to do it again while the second person derives a cynical joy from his act. The severity of the eventual consequence of the act is correspondingly stronger for the unrepentant, second person.

I was an avid collector of plastic buttons at age seven—I even ascribed names and imaginary personalities to some. The larger buttons were particularly useful. By threading a loop of cotton through the holes and alternately tensing and relaxing the tension of the cotton, the button to spun at great speed, producing a marvellous whirring sound. The larger the button, the better the sound. Somehow I acquired an enormous and elegant brown button, which emitted the best and loudest sound of all. But once my elder brothers discovered the powers of this singularly superior button it became an object of lust in their eyes. And so it came to pass one afternoon while I was playing happily with my button, they took it from me and refused to give it back. Soon I was in tears.

This attracted the attention of our mother, who demanded to know what we were fighting about.

"They took my button," I wailed, indignant at this new instance of the weak being tyrannised by the strong. My brothers of course denied everything, including the legitimacy of my claim to ownership of the button.

To my horror, my mother, instead of supporting my cause and administering justice on behalf of her youngest, as a mother should, took my beautiful button and smashed it with a hammer declaring,

"I'll teach you kids not to be so stupid as to fight over a button!" I was mortified. Rather than achieving instant illumination regarding the futility of materialism, I found my trust in parental justice sadly diminished.

> According to yoga psychology our personality, or ego-self, is nothing more than the sum total of the impressions in our mind, the Samskaras, waiting to gain expression.

A few years ago I reminded my eighty-year old mother of this incident. She did not remember it. Not because her memory was failing—far from it. The incident had little emotional impact on her. From her perspective it was just the boys fighting again, hardly something unusual. I'm sure my brothers remember it no more clearly than she. But I, shocked at the unfairness of my mothers 'solution,' was scarred for life. Well perhaps I'm getting carried away... maybe not for life, but you can see how an apparently insignificant incident like this can make a deep impression on a young child. At last my mother apologized, albeit 40 years later! But I still felt that her laughter showed a lack of appreciation for the gravity of the matter.

Through our lives, our emotional reaction to different situations are stored as impressions in our minds; these become potential reactions, known in Yogic terminology as Samskaras. Karma is the action, and the Samskara is the stored reaction. Often the word 'Karma' is mistakenly used in place of 'Samskara.'

According to yoga psychology our personality, or ego-self, is nothing more than the sum total of the impressions in our mind, the Samskaras, waiting to gain expression. They are who we are, or at least whom we think we are, to the extent that we identify with our ego. Our view of the world, our prejudices, beliefs and character traits, our complexes and strengths are all created by our past actions and thoughts. Our daily life is a complex interplay of our Samskaras. We usually experience this events caused by both impulses propelling us along in a relatively unconscious manner, and our free will driving us to initiate new thoughts and actions. Our accumulated Samskaras influence our present actions and thoughts, which in turn create new Samskaras as long as we remain identified with our ego. Even though we may be unconscious of it, this vicious cycle robs us of our freedom of choice. Eastern and Western psychology both have tools us to liberate ourselves from the binding influence of our Samskaras.

Making the Unconscious Conscious

Our Samskaras are, by their very nature, unconscious until activated by a thought or external stimulus. The reasons why we think and act in certain ways remain largely hidden until we actively seek them out. The majority of people today are far too 'busy' to take the time to uncover the hidden motives behind their actions. They are so caught up in the dynamic flow of their lives that they often imagine themselves to be the sole controllers of their world, never realizing to what extent they are driven by the accumulated momentum of their past thoughts and actions.

When people do awaken to the fact that they are the passive sufferers of their past conditioning, or more commonly, when some heavy reaction occurs which causes them great suffering in their life, they search for some means to liberate themselves from their psychic complexes. Lying on the psychologist's couch, they unburden themselves of their problems as the therapist guides them back down the corridors of memory to find what hidden traumas or experiences lie at the source of their current difficulties. A difficult and often painful process, the therapist and client endeavour to peel back the layers that lie between the client's conscious awareness and the stored impressions in the mind.

> *"Consciousness naturally resists anything unconscious*
> *and unknown... (we) erect psychological barriers to*
> *protect ourselves from the shock of facing anything new."*
> C.G. Jung

The latent force which is stored in an impression is often released

> It is important to remember that becoming conscious does not only involve gaining an intellectual understanding of oneself. The emotional energy that was stored in that impression must be experienced and released.

by the simple process of bringing what was unconscious into consciousness. Simply becoming aware of the original cause of our present anxiety is often enough to loosen its hold over us. The memory will remain, but the emotional power that was locked in that memory, the hidden tension associated with it that had so profoundly influenced our thinking and emotional state without our being aware of it, disappears. We may re-experience that energy with tears of pain as it is released, but once it is expressed, we feel free. It is as if we had released a fire-breathing dragon that had hunkered down in some dark corner of our mind, and we are now no longer a victim of its scorching breath. We relive the emotions associated with that forgotten or suppressed experience, and when we wake up the next day, we find that we are no longer afraid of snakes, or that our long unconscious resentment of our father has changed to a conscious understanding. It is important to remember that becoming conscious does not only involve gaining an intellectual understanding of oneself. The emotional energy that was stored in that impression must be experienced and released.

> "In the intensity of the emotional disturbance itself lies the value, the energy which he should have at his disposal in order to remedy the state of reduced adaptation. Nothing is achieved by repressing this state or devaluing it rationally."
> C.G Jung

An inescapable part of our personal development includes this journey into the dark forests of the mind to confront the demons and witches and dragons lying in wait. To chase them away with the light of awareness means a victorious return to full consciousness. This is the beginning of psychological freedom, which is nothing more than the awareness and release of these potential reactions or Samskaras. It can be a difficult and challenging journey, fraught with painful confrontations with our repressed desires, sorrows, and mental scars. But it brings with it the taste of freedom, the opportunity to become an increasingly conscious being whose choices are intentional, not those of a person who is just blown about by the winds of their past Karma.

As Jung has pointed out, there is nothing to be gained by avoiding our Samskaras—and everything to be lost. While this attitude of actively facing and working through our Samskaras can lead to some difficult lessons, those difficulties are nothing more than tollbooths on the road to freedom.

> "Your pain is the breaking of the shell that encloses your understanding.
> Even as the stone of the fruit must break, that its heart may stand in the sun, so must you know pain.
> And could you keep your heart in wonder at the daily miracles of your life, your pain would not seem less wondrous than your joy;
> And you would accept the seasons of your heart, even as you have always accepted the seasons that pass over your fields."
>
> Kahil Gibran

The Meditator's Approach

Western psychology relies on an analyst to help us explore the stored impressions from the past that affects our current life. The Yogic approach is somewhat different. Although it shares some essential elements with Western psychology and encourages us to take guidance from a spiritual teacher, it does not propose that the teacher should take the role of an analyst. Rather it encourages us to develop our own positive qualities and employ self-analysis.

On this point the two disciplines can be complementary.

A few years ago I spent a week alone in Switzerland for a personal retreat, staying by a beautiful lake. I spent hours in meditation, wrote music and practiced creative writing as a kind of self-analysis. Afterward, on a train going to Germany, writing about my experience, my mind was suddenly flooded with profound realizations about my own personality, my childhood, my relationship with my mother, and how these all influence my relationships with people even today. This insightful experience continued for about two hours. Although it was quite intense, I felt completely calm and by the end of it I was so much at peace with myself that I couldn't understand how I had ever felt disturbed by anything in my life. It was a wonderful experience; and certainly helped to resolve some deeply buried Samskaras of my own. It was strongly reminiscent of the realizations I imagine one is supposed to achieve from a series of sessions with a good psychoanalyst. Perhaps I should have sent myself a large bill!

In addition no second person acting as analyst, there is another fundamental difference between meditation and psychoanalysis: the goal itself. Western psychology is predominately concerned with releasing the unconscious elements of our mind that prevent us from leading a happy and well-adjusted life. It is not usually concerned with what lies beyond the mind or the deepest aspects of the Self. (There are notable exceptions. Brian Weiss, for example, used psycho-analysis as a stepping stone to meditation and spiritual experience.)

But for most people on a spiritual path this is not enough. They want it all. They want the jackpot—infinite happiness and the realization of their deepest Self. But if the mind is not balanced, the personality is full of unresolved complexes and we are driven by passions and addictions beyond our control, then reaching that state of supreme fulfilment remains as unlikely as the sun rising in the west. The deeper states of meditation stay forever beyond our reach. On this point the two disciplines can be complementary. Meditators recognize the need to free themselves from the Samskaras that keep them from their goal, and their meditation and associated practices become their means to achieve that.

In meditation we do not focus directly on our problems but gradually become aware of all our thoughts as they appear, while we focus our attention on the pure awareness from which these thoughts arise, the inner 'I' which lies behind all thoughts. Gradually we learn to be aware of the big picture, the nature of our individual mind and watch the thoughts arising from the well of Samskaras.

As we focus our mind on pure consciousness with the help of our Mantra, we become aware of the resistances and mental preoccupations that pull us away from our object of concentration. The deeper we go, the more we become concentrated on our inner awareness and the less we identify with the activities of the mind; slowly we become a silent witness to the mind. We recognize

> We become conscious of ourselves as an inner awareness, which transcends the turmoil and turbulence of our thoughts and desires. We find ourselves gradually drawn into the depths of an ocean of inner peace, completely undisturbed by the waves that ruffle its surface.

our issues as they reveal themselves with the intense clarity of a serene mind. We become conscious of ourselves as an inner awareness, which transcends the turmoil and turbulence of our thoughts and desires. We find ourselves gradually drawn into the depths of an ocean of inner peace, completely undisturbed by the waves that ruffle its surface. Dropping down into the silence of pure awareness, even if only for a moment, gives us the conviction that we will ultimately gain control over our restless minds and realize the tranquil Self within. And this inspires us to make greater and greater efforts.

Freeing the Mind from Samskaras

Through meditation, this practice of conscious awareness, the impressions stored in our mind express faster than through any other process, and the more so the deeper we go. It is as if we shine light into a dark room in search of the passageway leading to the freedom of the great outdoors. Meanwhile, the contents of the entire room are illuminated. Even beginning meditators become aware of a speeding up of the process of releasing Samskaras as their meditation progresses.

There may be no special effort to gain control over a particular desire or addiction, yet in our daily life we find it fading away of its own accord.

Or we wake up one morning and we realize that a particular fear or problem in our life is no longer an issue. What has happened is that the emotional energy locked up in that particular samskara has been released naturally in the process of our daily meditation. Meditation is not always easy because the ego resists our efforts to uncover what is hidden, but with time it is forced to admit defeat.

I suffered from extreme shyness as a child, and though I gradually overcame it during adolescence, it persisted when I played music. For more than 12 years I had a strong phobia about anyone hearing me play the piano. But within a year or so of learning meditation this fear simply dissolved. I didn't even notice its absence. I can now perform music before thousands of people with no problem.

Sometimes I notice people with a little tear in their eye when they meditate. After they finish their meditation they may not recall anything in particular that made them cry, but merely note an aware of the release of some emotional energy. Yogis call this process 'burning Samskaras.'

At other times a strong Samskara manifests itself quite directly when it is burnt. A friend had a young man in his meditation class who was gripped by an inexplicable fear whenever he stood ten and a half metres above the ground, yet he was otherwise unafraid of heights. At eight metres or at twelve he remained calm and collected. Then one day in his meditation the source of his peculiar phobia flashed in his mind. He had a memory of himself at four years old, dangling by one hand off a balcony ten and a half metres above the ground. He was smiling and calling to his mother. His mother screamed when she saw him hanging there and ran to pull him up to safety. He reported to the class that after recalling the incident in meditation his fear vanished.

> Meditators usually experience a speeding up of their external lives as potential reactions are uncovered and seek expression.

Often the potential reaction expresses itself in the form of something that happens to us. We may get hit by a car while crossing Main Street or lose our job through no fault of our own or win the lottery on a ticket that a friend bought for us. We have to undergo our Karma, good or bad, and that universal truth is reflected in the events of our life over which we seemingly have no control. Meditators usually experience a speeding up of their external lives as potential reactions are uncovered and seek expression. A whole lot more starts happening to us both externally and internally. We go through major changes. The unexpected comes up more often than it ever did before. On top of this, many Samskaras get dissolved in our meditation before they express themselves externally. As a result we experience the reactions purely in our minds, which is where all reactions are ultimately experienced, whether or not anything happens to us externally. In the same way all the actions that create Karma are really psychic actions, whether or not they get expressed on the material plane. Our lives become subtler as we are able to deal with our Samskaras on the emotional and mental level without having to learn our lessons in the school of 'hard knocks,' as the less conscious individual must.

In today's competitive world many still consider sitting quietly in meditation a fairly unproductive use of half an hour, but this couldn't be further from the truth. Not only does meditation free us from the past impressions, complexes and conditioning that prevent us from being a happy, healthy, well-adjusted, fully functional human being, it also takes us on a journey beyond into the supreme fulfilment of our innermost being.

"By 'activity,' according to modern usage of the word, is usually meant an action, which brings about a change in an existing situation through an expenditure of energy.

Thus a man is considered active if he does business, studies medicine, works on an endless conveyor belt, builds a table, or is engaged in sports. All these activities have in common the fact that they are directed towards an external, achievable goal. What is not taken into account is the motivation for the activity. Take for instance a man driven to incessant work by a sense of deep insecurity and loneliness or another one driven by ambition or greed for money. In all these cases the person is the slave of a passion, and his activity is in reality a form of passivity because he is driven: he is the sufferer, not the actor. On the other hand, a man sitting quiet and contemplating, with no purpose or aim except that of experiencing himself and his Oneness with the world, is considered to be 'passive,' because he is not 'doing' anything. In reality, this attitude of concentrated meditation is the highest activity there is, an activity of the soul, which is possible only under the condition of inner freedom and independence."

The Art of Loving by Erich Fromm

Mindfulness

The more we meditate, the more this reflective awareness becomes second nature to us, not only while we are meditating but also afterwards as we go about our daily activities. Rather than completely identifying with our ego and letting ourselves be simply carried away by the action or situation, we remain increasingly aware of our inner 'I,' the pure consciousness that is behind all our actions. We begin to notice how our mind acts and reacts in different situations. This quality of conscious awareness of our thoughts and actions is known as mindfulness.

By observing our mind, we become aware of the motivations behind our actions, thoughts and feelings. We may find ourselves in a situation which makes us angry, but rather than simply being carried away by the feeling and losing our temper, we watch our reactions as if we were watching a drama on a stage. This reflective observation reveals to

> We begin to notice how our mind acts and reacts in different situations. This quality of conscious awareness of our thoughts and actions is known as mindfulness.

us negative patterns in our mind, showing us how certain situations set off our anger like a trigger. We discover the causes behind the effects—a prejudice, a stored past hurt, a deeply imbedded fear. We mentally step back a little more, remember the tranquil consciousness that is our real self, and our anger dissolves almost as easily as it came.

Mindfulness teaches us compassion by showing us that we are ultimately responsible for both our actions and reactions. No one else makes us angry—just ourselves. We do that if we have the unexpressed Samskara for anger buried in our mind. Once that Samskara is released, however, challenging situations no longer have the power to 'make' us angry.

We may find ourselves at the receiving end of other people's inappropriate behavior and even take steps to rectify it, but it won't disturb our mental tranquillity. Even if we see that someone does something wrong, we feel compassion for them, because we see how they are driven by their Samskaras, just as we were (possibly) formerly driven by our Samskaras.

> This is sometimes known as detachment—letting go of our attachment to the results of our actions. We act, not because we want a particular result, but because it is the right course of action for that moment.

Buddha travelled with his monks from village to village, preaching the Dharma. He was an extremely charismatic, shining spiritual personality. Often whole villages became 'converted' to Buddhism due to His presence. In one village a young man, barely 13 years old, was so inspired he wanted to become a monk and leave his family to go with Buddha. His father, a farmer, was very angry and forbade him, but the boy ran away and joined Buddha's group. When the monks told Buddha He said, "Send him back to his family, he is too young." So they did.

But the boy ran away again, and followed Buddha's group, and again was sent back. He did this repeatedly until finally Buddha accepted him fondly saying, "How can we stop one who is so determined?"

One year later they returned to that village and the boy's father, the farmer, confronted Buddha, very angry. "You stole my boy away, you evil man. You are bewitching and corrupting our children and ruining lives. You black magician! Sorcerer! Child stealer!"

Buddha waited calmly for him to stop. Then He said, "If I offer you an apple, but you do not accept the apple, who has the apple?" The farmer was somewhat bewildered. He'd insulted this man and now he was talking about apples. He thought for a second. "I suppose you still have the apple, since I didn't accept it."

"That's right. Similarly, I do not accept these accusations and insults you have been so kind as to offer me, so they are yours." And Buddha smiled at the man.

What is Detachment?

As we develop concentration, our higher, intuitive mind develops more. We become wiser and less caught up in an ego-centric perspective. This is sometimes known as detachment—letting go of our attachment to the results of our actions. We act, not because we want a particular result, but because it is the right course of action for that moment.

Detachment is sometimes misunderstood as not caring about the world. This is a misconception. Detachment is freedom from egotism and selfishness, to step back and see our lives from a broader perspective.

"God please give me the strength to change those things I can change, the patience to endure those that I cannot, and the wisdom to know the difference."

Good luck? Bad luck? Who knows?

An old farmer in China had a horse helped him till his fields. One day the horse escaped. The old man's neighbors came by to sympathize with him over his misfortune, but all he had to say was: "Good luck? Bad luck? Who knows?"

The following week the horse returned with a herd of wild horses. This time his neighbors came by to congratulate him on his good fortune. Once again all he had to say was: "Good luck? Bad luck? Who knows?"

Not long afterwards, the farmer's son, while trying to tame one of the wild horses, fell off and broke his leg. The neighbors, of course, were convinced this was very bad luck indeed. Not the farmer, however. His reaction was the same as before. "Good luck? Bad luck? Who knows?"

War was declared in the country and some weeks later the army marched into the

As our meditation deepens and we develop our mindfulness, we discard old concepts of good and bad; and stop being upset when things don't turn out as we expected.

farmer's village to conscript every able-bodied young man. Because the farmer's son had a broken leg, they left him at home. Was it good luck? Bad luck? Who knows?

As our meditation deepens and we develop our mindfulness, we discard old concepts of good and bad; and stop being upset when things don't turn out as we expected. We learn the wisdom of Karma—that whatever happens to us is the result of our own actions—and we build our future on the firm ground of a deeper awareness of existence. We lose our egocentric way of thinking to accept the ups and downs of our daily life as natural. By learning to play the game of life in accordance with the laws of nature, of cause and effect, and recognizing that every action we perform has a reaction on the world, we develop a sense of responsibility and act in a way that benefits not only ourselves but everyone around us. And we tune in more and more to the unchanging consciousness from which all of experience arises, that blissful Self which transcends the world of actions and reactions.

> *"While watching a puppet show, you feel delighted to see how the puppets move their hands and feet, but you don't see the person who manages the beautiful show by pulling the strings from behind. Similarly, we notice the expressions of individual minds and we come to know how one sings melodious discourses, but we can't see the Entity who pulls the strings from behind and runs the show. And the funniest thing about it is this: the speaker, the singer, and the dancer all think that he or she is the agent, the doer, and takes the entire credit for the performance. That's why it has been said, 'One should be humbler than the grass.'"*
> Shrii Shrii Anandamurti

Ultimately love for the infinite Self within breaks us free from the chains of Karma. We leave the last of our limitations behind us and enter into an eternal peace that was always within us but which we have long forgotten. This is the end of a long road, and no matter how difficult the journey may have been, we realize that it was worth every step, when, for the first time, we open our eyes and see things as they really are.

Try This

•When you are meditating with the mantra, you may notice that different thoughts and feelings arise, and that they distract you.

•When a thought like this comes up, remember that your thoughts are not your enemies. They are the children of your own mind – you are creating them. So rather than treating them as something you must get rid of, simply remind yourself that they are also consciousness like everything else.

•To do this, when a new thought arises, just repeat mentally, Baba Nam Kevalam, and apply it to that thought or idea, as though you were touching the thought with a magic wand. Everything the mantra, your magic wand, touches turns to consciousness, something to be loved as an integral part of the Oneness that is within us.

•This can be especially effective when dealing with painful thoughts or memories.

•Record your experiences in your journal.

"*Train yourselves in the ideal of the lily, which blossoms in the mud and has to keep itself engaged in the struggle for existence day in and day out, parrying, bracing, and fighting through the shocks of muddy water and forces of storms and squalls and sundry other vicissitudes of fortune, and yet it does not forget the moon above. It keeps its love for the moon constantly alive. Prima facie however, it is but a most ordinary flower. There is nothing extraordinary about it. Still this most ordinary little flower is in a romantic tie with the great moon. It has kept all its desires riveted on the moon. Similarly, maybe you are an ordinary creature, maybe you have to pass your days in the ups and downs of your worldly existence, still, go deep into the feeling of that Infinite Love.*"

Shrii Shrii Anandamurti

Chapter Eight

Open Your Eyes

"A human being is a part of the whole, called by us 'universe,' a part limited in time and space. We experience ourselves, our thoughts and feelings, as something separated from the rest...a kind of optical delusion of our consciousness. This delusion is a kind of prison for us, restricting us to our personal desires and to affection for a few persons nearest to us. Our task must be to free ourselves from this prison by widening our circle of compassion to embrace all living creatures and the whole of nature in its beauty."
                              Albert Einstein

Once a spiritual teacher asked his student a question: "Why do you practice meditation?"

"To become a better person," was the disciple's simple response.

This seems like a good reply to me and it gives rise to further questions: What qualities should we seek to make us better people? Does meditation cultivate these qualities? What do we do when we open our eyes again—have we changed? Has our inner realization given us some fresh insight regarding our place in the world? How can we become more ideal human beings, not just in thought, but in action?

> What qualities should we seek to make us better people? Does meditation cultivate these qualities?

Some people question the social value of meditation and mysticism, suggesting that they can become a form of self-indulgence or selfishness, seeking personal happiness, but neglecting others. With so much suffering in the world, it seems reasonable to wonder whether we should devote so much time to our personal development.

If we were to meditate yet offer no comfort to others in their suffering nor spare a moment for selfless deeds, our development would be incomplete. Spiritual meditation does not allow this. It cultivates a sense of Oneness with all things and compassion for others. This feeling arises, not because of some theoretical idea that everything is connected, or because someone told us we ought to feel this way, but because it is the natural expression of our true nature.

Indigenous people, who live in close harmony with their natural environment, often feel this connection more readily than city dwellers.

> "Every part of the earth is sacred to my people. Every shining pine needle, every sandy shore, every mist in the dark woods, every meadow, every humming insect- all are holy in the memory and experience of my people."
> Chief Seattle

This marvellous feeling of connection with all life, when we are in the midst of its embrace, feels perfectly natural. So why don't we feel this all the time? What prevents human beings from feeling love for everyone in the world and constantly acting with selfless grace? To answer this question we need to understand how the ego forms egocentric or sentimental attachments.

Sentimental Attachment

If you ask a group of people what time it is, and they all consult their watches, often they'll all give slightly different answers. And if you ask them whose watch they think is right, you'll find that most people think their own watch is more likely to be right than someone else's. Why?

Because it is their watch.

What about our cars? Our houses? Our clothes? Are these not somehow more important than those of our neighbors? We associate our 'I' feeling not only with our minds and bodies, but with all manner of objects that we have identified as 'ours.' We identify with people in the same way. If a teacher criticizes your daughter, you leap to her defense, but you are unlikely to behave this way for another's child.

Your 'I' feeling is invested in your daughter.

In the comedy by Irish surrealist Flan O'Brien, The Third Policeman, a character propounds a theory about the remarkable relationship between policemen and bicycles. He maintains that whenever a policeman rides his bicycle, some bicycle molecules migrate to the policeman, and conversely, a number of policeman molecules merge with the bicycle, so that over time the bicycle becomes part policeman, and the policeman becomes part bicycle. If a policeman leans on a wall after the manner of a bicycle, it means he is already in serious danger of becoming more bicycle than policeman. And when bicycles mysteriously disappear from the place where they were left unattended, it is a clear indication that they are already part policeman.

This sure sounds surreal, but isn't this what we do a lot of the time?

Some portion of our 'I' feeling leaks into the things we own, so that we feel that a particular watch is 'my' watch. We can't bear to part with a favorite bedraggled item of clothing, or we develop an unnatural fondness for a beat-up and unreliable old car, or a deep attachment to another person. A little piece of the thing, or person, lodges in our minds, so that they occupy a corner of our mental world; if the thing gets lost, we feel lost: if the person is hurt, we feel hurt. If we are not careful, the possessor becomes the possessed.

> The problem is not that we love our own son or daughter too much. It is that we love everyone else too little. When we feel the same degree of love for all that we feel for our own children, we will be approaching 'God Consciousness.'

This 'sentimental attachment' is a tricky phenomenon. On the one hand it is human and perfectly natural to feel more love for one's daughter than for someone else's daughter. On the other hand, this natural sentiment easily become exaggerates and distorts, and we become over-attached. We become blind to our child's faults, or not allow her the freedom to become an independent adult.

The problem is not that we love our own son or daughter too much. It is that we love everyone else too little. When we feel the same degree of love for all that we feel for our own children, we will be approaching 'God Consciousness.'

Consider how these sentiments develop and affect our personal relationships and society as a whole.

The Evolution of Sentiment

Human beings are most attached to their own 'I' feeling. Our sense of 'I'ness defines who we are; it is difficult for us to see beyond this boundary. People often confuse body image with self-image. They think that they are their body. They haven't yet fully realized that their mental/emotional self is different from their physical self.

Because of this strong identification with the physical body, we identify more strongly with those objects or people in close physical proximity. We naturally feel closer to our family than we do to people living in a 'foreign' country.

This is what leads to the sentiment we feel for our tribe, race, country, religion, social class or species—it all depends on the degree to which our 'I' feeling associates itself with them.

In a small town Norwegian newspaper, a story about Mrs. Klem's cat stuck up a tree makes the front page, while an earthquake in Bahawulpur killing one hundred people is reported on page 37, just next to the week's supermarket specials.

Someone in my hometown in New Zealand produces a hit movie. I feel so proud. Why? I didn't make the movie. It is completely irrational, but I am from New Zealand, and that is the nature of sentiment.

Sentiment can be expressed in positive or negative ways. Identification with and pride in one's culture and language is an important factor in the development of one's identity and self-esteem. But when asserted as hatred or disregard for another race, class, religion, gender or species, it turns destructive. Nationalist, racist and religious sentiments give rise to a multitude of wars. Even in peacetime, many people accept the current situation where millions endure avoidable poverty and suffering while a few live in luxury. Why? Because 'those people' are not from our country or our tribe.

War will not end, and exploitation or oppression will not cease, while narrow sentiments prevail, pitting one group against another in competition and conflict. Only when we transcend these mental barriers of division and hatred will we create a society worthy of the name "civilization."

While speaking at a conference on Human Ecology, I pointed out that the root cause of our environmental crisis lives within us as flaws in human psychology with a lack of compassion and love for all living things. Another speaker expressed frustration that when a decision needed to be taken to avert ecological disaster, there was a 'lack of political will.' This simply means that the people with the decision-making power did not care enough to act. I replied that humans will behave responsibly, with love and compassion for all life, only when they undergo a change in consciousness. And meditation is a powerful tool to bring about that change.

humans will behave responsibly, with love and compassion for all life, only when they undergo a change in consciousness.

Later the conference chairman said, "I agree we need to get human beings to change their behavior, either through spiritual practice or through rational persuasion." He paused for a moment and then added a little ruefully, "The only problem is that rational persuasion doesn't seem to be working very well."

> "When the power of love overcomes the love of power, then the world will know peace."
>
> Jimi Hendrix

There is reason for hope. A brief glance back down the tunnel of history shows that in just a few hundred years we have come a remarkable distance on the path of moral evolution.

In the 17th Century, if you told someone that slavery would soon be illegal, they dismissed you as a dreamer.

In the 19th Century, if you predicted that in Europe within 100 years there would be universal suffrage, child labor eradication, universal free health care and education, and that businesses would have to submit themselves to environmental impact studies, they would have labelled you a utopian fantasizer.

In recent decades we've seen many significant advances: the collapse of political colonialism, the advent of the human rights movement, public demands for economic and social justice, the rise of environmentalism, and the unprecedented phenomenon of millions of individuals responding without hesitation to crises and natural disasters affecting strangers in far off lands.

We modern, educated humans are different creatures from our ancestors. Is it possible that we really are more enlightened than we once were? Our minds expand through education, travel, the media and exposure to different cultures; we are more aware of the importance of other lives and of our mutual interdependence. Never before in history has there been such widespread concern about humanitarian and ecological issues.

Before we pat ourselves too hard on the back it is worth remembering that many indigenous peoples are light years ahead of the Western world in terms of living in harmony with nature and one another.

Nevertheless we've made considerable progress in transcending racism, sexism

> We modern, educated humans are different creatures from our ancestors. Is it possible that we really are more enlightened than we once were?

and the various other forms of egocentrism that reflect the psychological root causes of 'man's inhumanity to man.' Yet we still have far to go. Time is running out as we face the greatest crisis of our planet. It is now a matter of urgency that we take the next step in our spiritual evolution.

To evolve further we must awaken our higher nature and remove the bitter seeds of hatred, greed and envy from our hearts. I know of no more powerful method to achieve this than the practice of meditation.

Spiritual meditation culminates in the experience of Oneness. In that state there is no sense of separation. Just as the sun's warmth touches every creature of the earth, so the love of an enlightened soul reaches out to embrace all, heeding no boundary.

> Just as the sun's warmth touches every creature of the earth, so the love of an enlightened soul reaches out to embrace all, heeding no boundary.

Relative Truth vs. Absolute Truth

Some Indian philosophers argue that the physical world is not real—it is an illusion, and therefore suffering is an illusion so there is no point in trying to do anything about it. Or that suffering is a result of people's bad actions or 'Karma' so attempts to help them are futile—that they have to experience it themselves in order to be free from the negative Samskaras. But this argument is neither logical nor compassionate.

Yoga philosophy proposes that although physical creation is not the ultimate and eternal reality, it does exist in a relative sense; from the point of view of its inhabitants, the world is all too real. If we have any moral sense or human feelings, the suffering of others should matter to us, just as it matters to them. And although it may be true that someone is suffering due to their past mistakes, it is equally true that we are being given an opportunity to remove our own negative Samskaras by helping them. When we have genuine spiritual feeling, we pause not an instant to consider these points. We feel that the infinite consciousness is appearing before us in the form of someone in pain, and help spontaneously.

> "Past the beggar and the suffering walks he who asks, 'Why, oh God, do you not do something for these people?' To which God replied, 'I did do something—I made you.'"
> Old Sufi saying

Someone once asked my spiritual master how to measure a person's spiritual progress? He replied, "You can only measure this by the periphery of their love."

If God is Love, and spirituality is the endeavour to allow God to flow through us, the more genuinely spiritual we are, the greater and more universal will be our love.

Law of Karma and Service

"Neither fire nor wind, birth nor death can erase our good deeds."
Buddha

Often when we do something for another person, we imagine that we are helping someone less fortunate than ourselves who is lucky to have us around. But in terms of Karma, the opposite is true. We are in fact the main beneficiaries of our own selfless deeds. The irony is that if our primary motivation is to reap good Samskaras for ourselves, rather than to relieve suffering, it will not have the desired effect. You may be able to fool yourself, or others, but it's a bit more difficult to pull a fast one on God.

"I slept and dreamt that life was joy. I awoke and saw that life was service. I acted, and behold, service was joy."
Rabindranath Tagore

One of my students related a personal problem. As it was not the first time he'd spoken to me about this, I became a little exasperated and said, "Why are you complaining? You're so lucky! You're a healthy, intelligent, highly qualified professional, earning heaps of money. You're good-looking, articulate, and you have plenty of friends. Your main problem is that you are always thinking about your own problems. Why don't you go somewhere where people aren't as lucky as you and help them? Why don't you go to a poor country and use your medical skills to help people with real problems?"

This was an uncharacteristic outburst on my part and I didn't expect him to take me literally, but I was pleasantly surprised when, a short time later, he told me that he was going to India to work as a volunteer. When he returned six months later I saw a remarkable change—he appeared much happier, and he told me, "Dada, I realized that the main person I helped all those months was myself."

"The best way to find yourself is to lose yourself in the service of others."

Mahatma Gandhi

"Love all, Serve all"

This is actually the slogan of the Hard Rock Café—a purely commercial enterprise as far as I can tell. The first time I noticed it on a big neon sign the irony struck me. "Serve them what?" I thought.

"Pizza and French fries?" Business is not service. Service means to give without expectation of anything in return. The term "service industry," seems contradictory.

"Do something for somebody every day for which you do not get paid."

Albert Schweitzer

Most people feel the desire and the need to help others in some way. We usually express this towards our loved ones, family, and friends...or our pet rocks. But we are also members of a greater family. All the living beings of the earth are children of the Supreme Consciousness. At a deeper level we are all connected. If others are in need, it is a sign of spiritual awareness that we feel the desire to help them.

> Most people feel the desire and the need to help others in some way.

Service can take many forms. There is no need to limit service to giving to charity or our immediate neighborhood. If we really want to help people, we must find out what they need and address that. There's no point in helping an old lady across the road only to discover that she didn't want to cross in the first place. And there is no point in trying to convince people to practice meditation when they don't even have enough food to eat.

There has been much debate in recent years about the effectiveness of aid work in developing nations.

Early efforts were adversely affected by a post-colonial patronizing attitude. Poor comprehension of local realities resulted in a string of expensive failures and the creation of long term dependencies. Tractors generously donated to villagers lay idle because of lack of spare parts or mechanical knowledge. Fertilizers or pesticides that the local people could not afford depleted soil that had been farmed organically for centuries. Rivalries, feuds and jealousies between different tribes were unintentionally fostered through lack of volunteer sensitivity and research. The list of mistakes and disasters clearly showed that it is all too easy, even with the best of intentions, to do more harm than good.

More recent aid and development efforts have proven more successful. Currently more aid workers make a conscious effort to understand the local culture, respectfully consult the local leaders and the community, and include the eventual goal of self-sufficiency.

But even this does not get to the root cause of poverty, which is often of economic injustice.

Take the example of current international trade policies. Trade rules today are skewed to such an extent that a cow in Europe receives more money via government subsidies than does an individual belonging to the poorest half of the population in Africa.

Poor countries have a lower share of world trade and it has dropped by almost half since 1981 and now stands (just barely) at only 0.4 percent. The United Nations estimates that if trade rules worked fairly for poor countries, they could reap benefits of up to US$ 700 billion a year—14 times the amount that developing countries receive in aid each year, and 30 times the amount they pay in debt repayments.

> a cow in Europe receives more money via government subsidies than does an individual belonging to the poorest half of the population in Africa.

In the long run, rather than giving direct charity to people in need, it is more effective to help them to become economically self-reliant. Here's the amazing story of how one man, starting with almost nothing, changed the economic circumstances of millions.

Muhammad Yunus founded the Grameen Bank in Bangladesh and later won the Nobel Peace Prize. Twenty-five years ago he was teaching economics at a University. There was a terrible famine in Bangladesh. He gave lectures on elegant economic theory and then walked past starving people on the way home. He then spoke to the local people to find out how they were living. An old woman who made bamboo stools earned only $0.02 per day because she had no money to purchase materials, while he trader from whom she got the materials demanded that she sell the stools to him at a low, low price. The bamboo for a stool cost about twenty cents. At first, Yunus considered just giving her the twenty cents, but then he got a bigger idea. He and a student collected the names of forty-two people in the village in the same position. The total needed to make them all independent of the exploitation of the trader was $27! So he gave this amount to them as a loan, saying they could repay it when they were able. When he approached the local banks, asking for their support in expanding the project, they refused, arguing that these poor people were not credit worthy and would not repay the money. But they did, so he added another village and another. After constant refusals by the banks to cooperate, he started his own "micro-credit" bank with the help of the Indian government.

Today the Grameen Bank is a community development bank working in more than 46,000 villages in Bangladesh and India. Since 2008, they loaned out more than $7.6 billion to the poor, with loans averaging less than $200 each. Their repayment rate is better than the commercial banks.

Muhammad Yunus, an economic theoretician by profession, didn't start this wonderful project with an elaborate theory or a plan. He simply saw a need and chose to act.

"Do all the good you can,
in all the ways you can,
for all the people you can,
for as long as you can."

John Wesley

How to Save the Universe

"We do not inherit the earth from our ancestors, we borrow it from our children."

Haida Indian saying

Long ago an old Wise Woman of the Cree Indian tribe named 'Eyes of Fire' had a vision of the future. She foresaw the coming of the white men; she saw that they would make war on her people, and on the earth, felling the trees, slaughtering the animals, poisoning the air and the waters. But in the last part of her vision she saw that a group of people would come together, from different tribes, different races, different nations and religions, and that they would make the earth green again. She called them the 'Warriors of the Rainbow.'

It certainly looks as if we are now living through the period she foresaw. We read about it in the newspapers every day. More of the Brazilian rainforest being felled, famine in Africa caused by drought and war, the growing water crisis, global warming causing weather patterns to change... and most of these problems can be traced to human activity.

"As a carry-over from our animal past, we have a territorial instinct, and tribal instinct. We are an emotionally, spiritually and morally undeveloped species with a highly

developed intellect and resulting technology. As tribes at least we had some sort of balance. But we have lost touch with our tribal roots, but not yet developed a more advanced system to replace it. As you know, this has led to a state where we are in danger of destroying our own environment. Already we have destroyed countless other species, and wreaked devastation on huge areas of our planet. We have set up a system which is so unjust that the wealth of a single man could prevent the deaths of millions of children, yet it is not used for this."

Conrad Lorenz

Many people understand that humanity is heading towards self-destruction, but feel powerless to prevent it. They go with their lives, trying not to think about it, or salving their conscience with regular donations to charity.

But we can do much more, even as small individuals. And if enough of us do what we can, we will change the world.

I am not going to go into detail about the vast range of options we have if we want to make a difference. That is a vast subject and this is not supposed to be a book about changing the world.

Yet in a way, it is. We are not islands. Every action we take, every thought that floats through our minds, every word we utter, creates waves that ripple outwards forever. An invisible power connects us all, and if we change ourselves, we will also change our world.

> Every action we take, every thought that floats through our minds, every word we utter, creates waves that ripple outwards forever.

"This we know: the earth does not belong to man, man belongs to the earth. All things are connected like the blood that unites us all. Man did not weave the web of life, he is merely a strand in it. Whatever he does to the web, he does to himself."

Chief Seattle

If our world is to be changed, it is people who will change it. People like you and me. People who are moved by a growing feeling of universal love, and a restless urge to do everything in their power to save our beautiful planet.

*"This is the true joy in life, being used for a purpose
recognized by yourself as a mighty one."*
George Bernard Shaw

John Robbins, heir to the vast fortune of the Baskin-Robbins
international ice-cream chain, made a critical choice some years ago.

In the course of facing and overcoming a serious illness, he underwent
a deep personal transformation. Emerging from his ordeal with a new
resolve, he renounced his position in the company and his share of the
family wealth and mounted a public campaign to make people aware of
the devastating effects of the meat industry in America.

Through his classic book, "Diet for a New America" and this Earthsave
Foundation, he educated millions of people and greatly influenced their
attitude towards health and the environment. (www.earthsave.org)

There is no need to go to Africa or
Bangladesh to serve our community.

Sometimes small things can change
people's lives. In the 1980s a woman in
Sydney, Australia became concerned about the
problem of loneliness amongst housewives in
her community. Suburban houses in Australia
are usually one- story homes with a small,
fenced backyard. She realized that all of the
fences kept people isolated. So she went to
all of her neighbors and proposed that they
remove all the fences in their block so that they
could easily meet and talk and their children
could play together safely away from the street
without anyone having to go out of the front
door. She had to be very persuasive, but in
the end everyone agreed, leading to a much
happier, safer and closer community. One person can make a difference.
There are literally millions of stories like this of individuals who are not
daunted by the forces opposing them, who are inspired by their vision of
hope and are acting to help create a brighter future for us all.

If you want to get a picture of the enormous scale of the present
worldwide movement for social change, I highly recommend reading
Blessed Unrest by Paul Hawken, where he documents the history of what
he describes as "the biggest social movement in the history of the world."

The Role of a Spiritualist in the World.

The rich spiritual tradition of yoga has profoundly influenced Indian culture since ancient times. This presents us with an apparent paradox. If yoga is so enlightening and practical, how come India is, in so many ways, such a poor example of what a spiritual society should be like?

It is a land plagued by inter-religious conflict, economic injustices, human rights abuses and casteism. It is hardly the shining Shangri La you might expect of the homeland of the glorious and transformational yoga tradition.

The sad truth is that in the arena of social justice, India has long since strayed from the Yogic ideal of "Dharma" symbolized by the wheel on her national flag. Although still clearly visible, India's high spiritual culture has been greatly undermined by the propagation of religious dogma, the divisive injustices of the caste system, and by waves of invasion and occupation, most recently by the Mughals and the British.

> yoga emphasizes the special duty of a spiritualist to set an example in society, and to help people to live more in accordance with spiritual values.

In addition to this, Indian Yogis retreat into ashrams or the Himalayas to meditate, neglecting the society of their birth. This became a 'spiritual brain drain,' where the very people who might have raised peoples consciousness, and popularized a more compassionate world view, chose to leave it all behind. This withdrawal is at variance with the original spirit of yoga, which advocates a balanced life, and does not suggest that we have to leave society in order to search for spiritual peace. Rather, yoga emphasizes the special duty of a spiritualist to set an example in society, and to help people to live more in accordance with spiritual values.

"All that is necessary for evil to triumph is for good people to do nothing."

Edmund Burke

I grew up during the Cold War and was involved in the peace movement from the age of five. Well, to be honest my parents were involved and I tagged along. At the ripe old age of twelve, I concluded that humanity was going to destroy the world through nuclear war, and I didn't see anything I could do about it. I stopped reading newspapers and took little interest in world affairs. I found the daily reports of human folly too depressing and I felt powerless to stop it.

Then when I was 19 years old I came to understand that there is a power in the Universe greater than any wielded by mere mortals and it awoke in me a great hope. I realized that I wanted to be a Yogi—I'd discovered something that gave my life a higher purpose—the spiritual path to self-perfection.

But I only felt my search complete when I found a philosophy that blended the Asian mysticism of yoga with the environmental and humanist philosophies from the West. I'd not only found personal meaning but my social conscience (never really dead, only resting) had re-awoken. I discovered fresh faith in the human spirit, in the innate goodness of human beings and in the power of individuals to make a difference.

> I only felt my search complete when I found a philosophy that blended the Asian mysticism of yoga with the environmental and humanist philosophies from the West.

Imaginal World

Imaginals are the unique cells that transform caterpillars into butterflies, which I think is pretty poetic for a scientific term. This is becoming a popular metaphor for the transformation of our world into a place of love, justice and harmony.

I believe that we can all become Imaginals, and like a billion brilliant cells inspired by love, we can use our creative powers to bring about an era of peace and goodwill on Earth. In fact, it is already happening.

> we can all become Imaginals, and like a billion brilliant cells inspired by love, we can use our creative powers to bring about an era of peace and goodwill on Earth

Here are a couple of many human Imaginals I know:

A Norwegian friend has spent many years building water supplies for poor areas in Ghana. The project now supplies fresh water to more than 16,000 villagers, and has completely transformed their lives. Now the villagers manage and maintain everything themselves. My friend lives in difficult physical conditions unimaginable for most Norwegians, but he insists that this is the happiest time of his life.

http://www.africa.amurt.net/ghana/

Another colleague from Australia started a children's home in

Mongolia years ago. She now cares for more than 100 abandoned children.

http://www.anandamarga.org/service/childrens-homes2.htm

These people did not start out with a lot of money or special skills.

A true Imaginal is possessed of something far more valuable—a feeling of universal love and a willingness to sacrifice their comfort, energy and time for others. With this spirit, even one person can make an enormous difference.

Perhaps you know some Imaginals too. After all, anyone can become an Imaginal, even you.

> *"We are not powerless specks of dust drifting around in the wind, blown by random destiny. We are, each of us, like beautiful snowflakes – unique, and born for a specific reason and purpose."*
>
> Elizabeth Kubler-Ross

The Beautiful Revolution

> *'Building anything on humanistic lines requires a foundation of real love for humanity. A truly benevolent society will never come into being under the leadership of those who are solely concerned with profit and loss. Where love is paramount, the question of personal loss and gain does not arise. The basic ingredient for building a healthy society is simply love."*
>
> Shrii Shrii Anandamurti

There exists a type of 'service' that is not always appreciated but may have the most far-reaching effects of all. If we help others to realize their spiritual potential, to awaken their love for humanity, it rouses a force that does not fade, but grows and multiplies, spreading good will and good deeds through immeasurable time.

Think about it. You or I alone can only do so much. But if we can foster in others the awareness that they are members of a universal family, and if sufficient numbers come to feel this in their hearts, we could create a veritable heaven on earth.

> *"You see things that are; and you ask, 'Why?' But I dream things that never were; and I ask, 'Why not?'"*
>
> George Bernard Shaw

I taught meditation to a man who had been involved in radical politics his entire life, starting out in the communist party and later migrating to the peace movement. A good-hearted man, he was eager to alleviate human suffering. He felt that it was important to address the causes of our problems—to find a long-term solution. Learning meditation was a considerable departure from his normal way of thinking. We became engrossed in a profound discussion, and I spoke to him of the Beautiful Revolution. The Beautiful Revolution envisages a society that promotes human welfare, enlightenment and lasting happiness: education systems redesigned to turn learning into a joy rather than a chore; culture restored to its proper place as an aesthetic and inspirational pursuit, rather than a mere avenue of commerce; social, economic, and political institutions recast in a nobler role as means to ensure justice for all and instruments for the formation of an ecologically sustainable society based on humanitarian and spiritual values.

> I still remember the expression of wonder on his face as he said, "Now that is really revolutionary."

Our discussion ranged far and deep, as we considered what the world would be like if we could only treat one another as members of our own family. As we finally emerged from our beatific vision my new friend looked at me in amazement. I still remember the expression of wonder on his face as he said, "Now that is really revolutionary."

"The flame of a lamp lights up countless lamps. The touch of a great personality wakes up innumerable sleeping hearts. In the same way, the eternal glow of the boundless élan vital of Cosmic Consciousness has been illuminating the life-lamp of universal humanism since time immemorial, is illuminating it, and will do so in future even more intensely. That is why I say, the future of the human race is not dark, rather it is strikingly resplendent. So proceed on, ignoring the frown of darkness."

Shrii Shrii Anandamurti

Try This

Close your eyes and imagine that you are a single cell in the great body of humanity. Humanity is evolving – striving to express it's limitless potential for love and awareness. As a self aware, intelligent, Imaginal Cell, you can contribute to this awakening. Through the way you live, you can create something beautiful for all to share.

Ask yourself, what is my role in this process of awakening as our amazing species takes its first infant steps into a new Era of Peace, Love and Justice?

Think about it for some moments. Let your imagination run free – do not limit yourself with ideas of what may or not be possible – let your vision unfold with no boundaries. Take your time.

Open Your Eyes

Write your thoughts in your journal.

You may wish to send what you have written to someone who is close to you. I'd be honoured if you were to send some of your Imaginal thoughts to me. But most importantly, keep it for yourself, and refer back to it for your own inspiration. Often.

Samgacchadvam

'Let us move together. Let us sing together. Let us come to know our minds together. Let us share, like sages of the past, that all people together may enjoy the universe. Unite our intentions, let our hearts be inseparable, our minds are as one mind, as we, to truly know one another become one."

Rig Veda (12,000 BCE)

Appendix A:
Next Steps on Your Journey

Learning to Meditate

Where do you go from here? You have several options. You could: read some more books; attend a meditation class; start practicing meditation right away; find a personal teacher. If you are inspired to start practicing now, you should go ahead. But I believe that to get the best results in meditation you need personal instruction, so my recommendation is to find a teacher who guides you in the principles of meditation. However, if you aren't able to do that, here is something you can try until you meet the right teacher.

Introductory Meditation Technique

In the Ananda Marga meditation system we generally use a personal Mantra. However, there is a universal Mantra that we teach as an introductory technique. The Mantra consists of three Sanskrit words:
   Baba Nam Kevalam.

- **Baba** means 'beloved' and it refers to your deepest Self, the Infinite Consciousness or Supreme Consciousness.
- **Nam** means 'name' or 'vibration' and
- **Kevalam** means 'only.'

The literal meaning of the Mantra is 'Only the name of the Beloved,' but some people find it easier to focus on the implied or inner meaning of the Mantra i.e. that everything is an expression of Infinite Consciousness, and that our own consciousness is are reflection of That.

Or more simply, Love is All There Is, or All is One.

Try to feel that Infinite Consciousness is all that exists, and that its nature is perfectly loving, blissful and peaceful. Feel that there is nothing and no one closer to you than that perfectly loving Entity. It is important to keep the idea of the Mantra in your mind while you repeat the Sanskrit words: **Baba Nam Kevalam**. To get a clearer idea of this take a look back at the chapter on Mantra..

Probably the easiest way to get into your meditation will be to use the guided meditation recordings included with this book.

Sit comfortably with your back straight. If you can sit comfortably on the floor, perhaps with a cushion, I'd recommend that. Play the recording, and close your eyes and follow the guided meditation. As you become more habituated in your practice you might want to start doing it without the guided meditation part of the recording, but it is always good to listen to or sing the mantra before meditation.

If your mind wanders to other thoughts, just bring it back to the Mantra, and if it wanders again, bring it back again. Remember what I said about training a dog? Repetition is the key.

When thinking about the meaning of the Mantra it usually helps to focus more on the feeling than on the thoughts. I often tell my students, 'Don't think, just feel.' Infinite Consciousness is a mind-expanding idea, but it can sometimes seem too abstract. Try this. Remember that all the love, peace and happiness you've ever felt come from within you. Your object in meditation is to connect with the source of the feelings that give our lives meaning. You are not meditating on anything other than you own innermost Self.

Do the meditation two times a day. In the morning after waking up, sit for meditation. In the evening, just before the evening meal, sit for meditation again. If you can get into the daily routine of doing meditation, you are on the way to success.

I must however emphasise that it is far better and easier to grasp meditation if you have the encouragement and guidance of an experienced teacher and practice with a group. If you want to contact the nearest Ananda Marga meditation center, go to www.anandamarga. org where you can find the locations in your part of the world.

Feel free to write to me at nabhaniilananda@eternalwave.com

Appendix B:
Practical Tips to Improve Your Meditation

1. Minimize interruptions

Switch off the bell on your phone, let your friends and family know that during this time you desire no interruptions; close the door, close your eyes and leave the ordinary world behind. This has tremendous psychological impact. If, while meditating, one part of your mind is listening for the doorbell, or is ready to jump up if the phone rings, or to come out if someone wants to talk, it will be very difficult to concentrate. Give yourself completely to the task, letting the people around you know that it is important to you. They will learn to respect it too. Establish immediately that during this period of time you do not wish to be disturbed, making whatever arrangements are necessary (childcare trade-offs, phone message arrangements, etc.) and you will feel freer and happier in your meditation.

2. Meditate at the same time of day

Experienced meditators find that if they always meditate at, say, 6am and 5:30 pm, when that time of day occurs they naturally want to meditate. Optimum times are around sunrise and sunset. The effect of the Mantra on a deeper level carries over for about 12 hours, so if you meditate twice a day the subtle effect of the Mantra carries on all the time.

If one sincerely desires to explore meditation it is important to establish a habit of regular meditation. Twice daily is best: in the morning to tune in and charge up to start the day, and in the evening to establish rhythm and harmony in your life. This twice a day meditation ties us in with the world's daily rhythms. It is important to maintain this regularity.

People who are beginning meditation frequently report having difficulty finding the time to meditate. Writing out your daily schedule and then 'brain-storming' (figuring out possibilities and listing as many as you can) all sorts of different ways to make time may help to get over this hump. Experienced meditators frequently report a considerably reduced need for sleep (due to the deep state of physiological rest during meditation) and so may gain as much as 1-3 hours of usable time.

3. Twice a day, invariably

This is the key to success in meditation. If one sincerely desires to explore the heights and depths of meditation, it is important to establish a habit of never missing your practices. Meditation can be likened to a beautiful chain—each day we add delicate links; the overall effect is a strong and useful instrument. But if we miss a meditation we create a 'missing link.' To make the mind strong, try to never miss a session. Be uncompromising. Even in an emergency, it is possible to perform your meditation for five to ten minutes. It may take an effort at first, in the long run it becomes second nature like brushing one's teeth.

4. Meditate in the same place

Try to arrange a corner or even a small room for your meditation space. Keep it clean and fresh and try to do your meditation there all the time. You will find this special place develops deep meaning for you. When you go to this space in your mind, you will naturally want to meditate. You can really feel this if you meditate in a place where a great Yogi has practiced their meditation for many years. Of course you can meditate anywhere in an office or a car, on the bus, outside—but it helps, especially in the beginning to have a quiet and special place dedicated to meditation.

5. Meditate on a light stomach

After eating, the energies of the body are directed toward the digestive processes at the expense of the mental (think of the sluggishness that follows a heavy meal). Because meditation requires alertness, concentration, mental energy and 'wakefulness' it is helpful to meditate on an empty stomach. If you are really famished take a glass of juice or milk or eat lightly. If your body is really hungry, your meditation may be distracted.

6. Meditate in a comfortable, erect posture

When meditation proceeds properly, there is a flow of energy upwards through the spinal column. Slumping or slouching impedes this energy flow, impairs breathing and diminishes mental alertness.

So it is important to sit as straight as possible. A firm surface is helpful. Gentle stretches or warm-ups help prepare the body for meditation. Some people find that putting a small pillow underneath their seats alleviates pressure on the knees and induces better posture by elevating the spinal column.

It is important to be comfortable so that your mind is free to concentrate on the meditation process. If sitting on a rug, cushion or folded blanket is not comfortable, you may want to meditate sitting in a chair. With twice daily practice of good sitting posture and some stretches and warm-ups to loosen the body, most people are amazed to discover how relaxed and flexible they can become in just a few weeks time.

7. Keep good company

One of the greatest supports through the ups and downs of your spiritual growth is time spent with others who are walking the path of meditation. Weekly group meditations are extremely important for the serious meditator.

Ananda Marga conferences, classes and seminars offer meditators a chance to meditate with others and immerse themselves in their spiritual practices and learn more about the philosophy of yoga.

8. Read spiritually elevating books

The intellect, which hopefully keeps quiet during meditation, also needs scope for growth and development. Therefore, it is recommended that one set aside some time each day for reading spiritually uplifting books. After meditation take a few minutes for reading, as the mind is clear and calm and more easily absorbs ideas. Appendix D includes a recommended reading list.

9. Talk to a meditation teacher

I am one of more than 1200 teachers who work with the Ananda Marga spiritual movement. Ananda Marga means 'The Path of Bliss' and it is an association set up for the purpose of propagating the practices of meditation, yoga and social service. Find out more about it on the website www.anandamarga.org. A teacher in this system is known as 'Acharya' which means 'one who teaches by example.' If you talk to an Acharya you get answers to your questions about meditation and personal instruction, free of charge. Local members of Ananda Marga know when Acharyas are expected to visit, and what kind of activities are planned (lectures, group meditations, etc.) while they are visiting.

10. Persevere

Experiences vary in the beginning of meditation. Some enjoy it immediately, others may feel discouraged or frustrated if the results of their first few meditations do not measure up to their expectations or hopes. They may feel that it is their own fault, and even give up the practice with a sense of failure or inferiority. Every meditator deals with this in some way. It is a great help to know that others may also be having similar experiences and to understand what is actually taking place during this time.

Especially in the beginning, the mind may seem uncontrolled. The great Yogi Ramakrishna, once said: "The mind is like a drunken monkey stung by a scorpion." You may find when you sit down to meditate that many thoughts arise in your mind; you set your Mantra going and then drift off to something else. Sounds and noises side track your internal concentration and your body becomes restless. At times like this, one can easily get discouraged and think nothing is happening. However, many of the benefits of meditation come from deep within the mind and do not show themselves immediately. By constantly bringing your mind back to the Mantra, you are building up your capacity to hold your mind steady in the future. If you have the determination to pass through any initial difficulties you will be richly rewarded.

Reprinted with permission of Ananda Marga

Appendix C:
Astaunga Yoga – Eight Steps to Perfection

The goal of Tantra Yoga is complete happiness and the method for attaining it lies in the full development of mind, body and spirit.

Animals develop naturally through the evolutionary process, but for self-aware human beings, Tantra prescribes a well-defined method to accelerate our development. There are eight parts of this practice and since its goal is union (yoga) with the Cosmic Consciousness, it is also known as Astaunga Yoga, or Eight-Limbed Yoga.

The first two steps are Yama and Niyama, which are a set of ten ethical principles for human development. The idea here is that by controlling our behavior we achieve a higher state of being. The idea is not simply to follow a rule for its own sake; rather the object is to attain perfection of the mind. When this state of perfect equilibrium is attained then there will be no question of 'rules' because the desire to do harm will no longer be present in the mind.

1. Yama: ethical guidelines

Ahimsa: 'Do no harm to others in thought, word and actions.' This principle is sometimes interpreted to mean complete non-violence, but in fact this is impossible to follow if taken literally. For example each time we breathe we inhale and kill microbes. In order to live, we have to eat something living. In this case, the spirit of Ahimsa is to select organisms whose consciousness is least developed, rather than killing highly developed creatures.

Another question that arises is that of the right to self-defense. Ahimsa says that to defend one self, or another, against an aggressor is justifiable. Even if you use force, your intention is to save and protect life, not to cause harm.

Satya: 'Action of mind and the use of speech in the spirit of welfare.'

This means to tell the truth and act to promote the welfare of all. In cases where telling the literal truth will harm others, then Satya means we should say what is best for the welfare of others, whether or not it is the literal truth. Adherence to Satya brings about tremendous strength of mind and is extremely important for spiritual success.

Asteya: 'Non-stealing.' This means not take another's possessions— or to even contemplate the same. Those who want to steal but refrain from doing so out of fear of being caught are 'mentally' stealing. Asteya means to refrain from both mental and physical stealing.

Brahmacarya: 'To remain attached to Brahma (the Cosmic Consciousness) by treating all beings and things as an expression of the Cosmic Consciousness.' The mind takes the shape of the object of our thought. If we perform all actions, remembering that everything in this world is actually the Cosmic Consciousness in a transformed state, then the mind will move towards a state of Oneness with the Cosmic Consciousness. In some books Brahmacarya has been described as sexual abstinence, but this a distortion of the idea that was propagated in the Middle Ages by Hindu priests who wanted to attain supremacy over ordinary family people.

Aparigraha: 'To not hoard wealth, which is superfluous to our actual needs.' Live a simple life with only as much physical wealth as is actually necessary. It is an important principle in both individual and collective life, because if one person or one nation hoards wealth, it may result in shortage and misery for others. It helps spiritual practice, because it frees the mind of preoccupation with material objects.

2. Niyama: self-regulation

Shaoca: 'Purity of mind and body.' It includes cleanliness of one's external world such as the body, clothing and environment, as well as the internal world of the mind. Purity of thought can be attained by autosuggestion—substitution of a good thought in place of a negative thought.

Santosa: 'To maintain a state of mental ease.' Desire creates a state of uneasiness. Upon satisfying that desire, the moment of relief we feel is called tosa in Sanskrit. Those people who are easily satisfied and remain contented are following Santosa.

Tapah: 'To undergo hardship on the path of personal and collective development.' Acting in the spirit of service to others without expecting anything in return is Tapah. In the past some spiritual aspirants practiced self-inflicted hardships and austerities (like walking on fire) but such austerities do not provide benefits to the aspirant, to the society or to Cosmic Consciousness, so they are not helpful in spiritual advancement.

Svadhyaya: 'Having a clear understanding of a spiritual subject.' One should read and assimilate the meaning of great books and scriptures written by spiritually advanced people. Mere reading without understanding is not Svadhyaya. The importance of Svadhyaya is that it gives us contact with great personalities and inspires one to continue on the path of self-realization.

Iishvara Pranidhana: 'To make the Cosmic Consciousness the goal of our life.' This is done through spiritual meditation.

3. Asanas: yoga postures

Asanas are postures comfortably held. This is the most well known part of yoga, but their purpose is often misunderstood. Asanas are not the same as calisthenics or gymnastics. They regulate the functions of the body, affecting the endocrine glands, internal organs, joints, muscles, ligaments and nerves. Properly prescribed, they are used in the prevention of many mental and physical diseases and their regular practice slows the aging process. They are intended to maintain flexibility and good health, and by balancing our hormonal secretions create a state of mental balance and calm, preparing the body for meditation.

4. Pranayama: control of vital energy

Pranayama is a well-known practice of yoga, but the principle upon which this practice is based is not widely understood.

Tantra defines life as the parallelism of physical and mental waves in proper coordination with vital energies. The vital energies are known as vayus or 'winds.' There are ten vayus in the human body which are responsible for the moving activities including respiration, circulation of the blood, excretion of wastes, movement of limbs, etc. The controlling point of all these vayus is an organ known as pranendriya. (The pranendriya, like the Chakras, is not an anatomical organ.) This pranendriya also has the function of linking the various sensory organs with a point in the brain. The pranendriya is located in the center of the chest and it pulsates in synchronization with the process of respiration.

When there is a rapid pulsation of the breath and also of the pranendriya, it is more difficult for the mind to link up with sensory perceptions. For example, if you run a race of 1,000 meters you cannot immediately eat something and recognize the flavor of what you have eaten due to the rapid breathing and disturbed functioning of the pranendriya. During rapid breathing it becomes more difficult to concentrate.

Advanced pranayama exercises involve a special breathing process in which the pulsation of the pranayama becomes still and the mind becomes calm. This helps meditation. Pranayama also readjusts the balance of vital energy in the body. Advanced Pranayama exercises, including alternate nostril breathing and retaining the breath, can be dangerous if not taught with the guidance of a competent teacher. These should not be practiced by beginning meditators.

5. Pratyahara: sense withdrawal

Withdrawing the mind from its attachment to external objects is an important step towards deep meditation. With regular meditation practice it can take you to a state of profound inner peace.

6. Dharana: concentration

In personalized meditation techniques, the practitioner is taught to concentrate on a particular point—this helps greatly in focusing the mind. There are also more advanced methods of dharana taught in Tantra, which involve concentration on different points and colors. These techniques help the meditator to gain control over the mental propensities governed by the different Chakras, as well as increasing concentration.

7. Dhyana: spiritual meditation

There are different forms of dhyana. When Tantric teachers from India first brought this technique to China it became known as Chan, and when Chan was brought to Japan via Korea, it ultimately became known as Zen. Although there are important differences between contemporary Zen meditation and dhyana as practiced by the Tantric masters in India, the root teaching was the same. Dhyana helps to perfect the most subtle layer of the mind and leads the person to the final step of Astaunga Yoga which is samadhi.

8. Samadhi: spiritual trance

Samadhi is not like the other seven steps in that it is not a particular method or practice, rather it is the result of practicing the other parts of Astaunga Yoga. It is the absorption of mind in the Supreme Consciousness. There are two principal forms of Samadhi, Nirvikalpa and Savikalpa. Savikalpa is a trance of absorption with distortion or qualification. In Savikalpa Samadhi the person has the feeling that 'I am the Supreme Consciousness,' but in Nirvikalpa Samadhi there is no longer a feeling of 'I.' The individual consciousness is totally merged with the Cosmic Consciousness.

Those who experience Nirvikalpa Samadhi are not able to explain or describe it because it occurs when the mind has ceased to function. The only way they can even know that they have experienced this state is after the mind returns from this trance of absorption. Then they experience waves of extreme happiness and understand that they were in the state of Nirvikalpa Samadhi. The attainment of Nirvikalpa Samadhi comes after millions of years of evolution, and prolonged spiritual effort.

It is the final merger with the source of all being and the ultimate goal of meditation.

Adapted from The Wisdom of Yoga by Acarya Vedaprajinananda Avadhuta

©1990 Ananda Marga Publications, all rights reserved.

Appendix D:
Recommended Reading List

Some of My Favorite Books

Here is a selection of books on meditation, mysticism and spirituality.

Some of these are biographies or novels rather than philosophical works.

Available from www.anandamarga.org

Elementary Philosophy – Shrii Shrii Anandamurti
Beyond the Superconscious Mind – Didi Ananda Mitra

Generally available through mainstream distributors such as www. amazon.com

Anandamurti – The Jamalpur Years by Devashish Acosta
The Unity Principle by Steven Richheimer
Autobiography of a Yogi – Paramahansa Yogananda
Siddhartha – Herman Hesse
God's Pauper (biography of St Francis of Assisi) - Nikos Kazantzakis
Milarepa, Tibet's Greatest Yogi
No Boundary – Ken Wilbur
The Tao of Physics – Fritjof Capra
Zen Mind, Beginner's Mind – Shunryu Suzuki
Ramakrsna: Life of Ramakrsna – Christopher Isherwood

Websites to check out:

www.themonkdude.com

This is my personal website where you can find more about my books, my music and my spiritual teaching work.

www.imaginalworld.com

This is my interview site where I speak to some of todays leading spiritual and creative progressive thinkers.

Glossary of Sanskrit Terms

Atman: Individual soul or consciousness.

Cakra or Chakra: Controlling point of glands and vital energy of the body. There are seven major chakras along the spinal column. These are also the meeting points of the flow of vital energy flowing through the body.

Karma: Literally means 'action;' often confused with 'samskara.' Karma is often confused with the Law of Karma, which pertains to action and reaction.

Kundalinii: latent spiritual potential of the individual. It normally resides dormant at the base of the spine until the time of spiritual awakening. It is often represented in the shape of a coiled snake.

Mantra: A word or group of words, that when repeated aloud, or mentally during meditation, facilitates the awakening of spiritual awareness. The mantra is only really effective if the meaning is also kept in mind.

Paramatman: Supreme soul or consciousness, the role of witness of the universe.

Prana: Life force or vital energy called Chi in Chinese, or Ki in Japanese. The three main channels through which Prana flows run along the spine, one straight up the center, and the other two starting behind each nostril and weaving their way back and forth across the spine, crossing at each of the 5 lower Chakras.

Samadhi: Trance of absorption, the individual mind merges with the Cosmic Mind.

Samskara: Potential reaction to one's own experiences and actions, stored in the mind. Often confused with 'Karma.'

Sanskrit: Ancient language of the Vedas, which is composed of the fifty sounds that correlate to the fifty vrittis of the human mind. Meditation mantras are usually in the Sanskrit language.

Vrittis: Mental propensities. There are 50 desires, emotions and tendencies of the human mind: love, hatred, shame, anger, fear, sorrow, hunger, spiritual longing, to name a few.

Guided Meditation
CD Download

Sunrise Meditation and Sunset Meditation,
including kiirtan chanting music
and guided meditation.

To download these two MP3s for free go to

www.themonkdude.com/guidedmeditation

enter your name and email,

and the link will be automatically forwarded to you.

New Meditation Home Study Course
Special Offer

I've been using the material in this book to teach classes for a long time, and I've received many requests for a workbook to help people who want to start practicing meditation every day at home. I'm excited to announce that I have just completed the Close Your Eyes & Open Your Mind Meditation Home Study Course.

This package includes:

- The "Close Your Eyes open your Mind" book

- A 100 page workbook comprising 8 modules
  one for each chapter - full of exercises and assignments to help you to get started meditating regularly.

- A series of 8 guided meditation recordings on 4 CDs.

- An audio version of the Close Your Eyes & Open Your Mind book.

- The perfect music to create the mood for your meditation.
  These are my personal favorites from incredible Norwegian guitarist Sukha Deva. I think it is the most beautiful spiritual chanting CD in the world!

If you're inspired to act on what you've read in this book by making meditation a daily practice, this Home Study Course is designed for you.

Special Offer:
As a gift for my readers I'm offering a $50 discount on the course!

Please visit:

www.themonkdude.com/store/MHSC/specialoffer1

CPSIA information can be obtained
at www.ICGtesting.com
Printed in the USA
BVHW07s1057060818
523682BV00003B/165/P